Year of the Babies!

Year of the Babies!

A Journey Through Loss, Childlessness, Adoption, and Cancer

Anne Van Donkersgoed

Dedication

This book is dedicated to
Gracie, Emma, & Sarah.
You have brought
great joy
into my life!

Acknowledgements

I would not have had the courage to print this book if it had not been for the encouragement and support of my husband. He has walked beside me and supported me through this journey. Ed brings confidence, joy, and love to my life. Thanks Ed!

I would like to thank my friend, Sue Loomis, for critically reading my draft copy of this book and making many useful suggestion and corrections. I trusted Sue because she is one of the few people who knows my heart. She has been a tremendous support over many years. Thank-you Sue.

Thank-you to my brother John, for helping me get this book to print. Your willingness to do so means a lot to me.

Contents

Introduction

This book journeys through my life from the first weeks of my marriage to the current day. It wanders through my thoughts and feelings of losing babies and miscarriage. It gives a glimpse of my years of being childless and how I was blessed through the lives of other people's children. It tells the adoption stories of my three girls. Finally it gives a very personal account of my life as the mom of a baby with cancer. I trust you will laugh with me, cry with me, and rejoice with me as you read my story. I pray you will get a sense of a life with many ups and downs but with the thread of faith in God running through it all.

* Some names have been changed to protect their privacy.

IWK – Isaak Walton Killam Children's Hospital, Halifax NS

KCMH – Kings County Memorial Hospital, Montague PEI

QEH – Queen Elizabeth Hospital, Charlottetown PEI

EMS – Emergency Medical Services, ambulance

PICU – Paediatric Intensive Care Unit

PEI – Prince Edward Island, Canada

www.yearofthebabies.com

1. The Beginning

This story begins just after Ed and I were married. It starts on a Saturday morning in January, 1985, when I had an interesting conversation with my father-in-law, Bert.

Ed and I had arrived at his parents' home for a visit. Bert told Ed not to take off his coat. He wanted Ed to drive his Mom, Mynie, shopping. I thought I'd go along too but Bert said no. He said I was to stay at the house. Mynie said she did not need to go shopping but he replied, yes you do and here is the list and money. I was feeling *very* uncomfortable. I didn't know my father-in-law very well.

Ed and Mynie left to go shopping and Bert made me a cup of coffee. He said we needed to talk. We sat in the living room, across from each other, drinking our coffee. He was quiet for a while and then cleared his throat to speak. I could not have imagined the words that came from his mouth! He informed me that he wanted to be a grandfather and wanted to know what I was going to do about it! I turned beet red, gasped, and replied that maybe he should talk to Ed. He responded that of course he couldn't talk to Ed about such things, that's why he was talking to me. I told him I would keep him posted!

Ed and I had discussed having children and had decided that we would take them when they came. We planned to start with several of our own children and then make a home for foster children or possibly adopt. I was fairly certain when Bert was talking to me that I was already pregnant but I didn't tell him.

By January 18, 1985, Ed and I had been married for about 5 weeks. My oldest sister Ruth, was visiting for a few days on her way from Prince Edward Island to Vancouver. She had never met Ed's parents and so we had planned a potluck supper at their home in Listowel. His two brothers, his sister, and his brother-in-law would all be there. On the drive up Ed said he wanted to tell his Dad I was pregnant but I wanted to wait a few more weeks. We enjoyed a meal and visit with our family and then returned home to Guelph. That was a Friday.

The following Monday evening we were sharing a meal with three of Ed's cousins when we received word that Bert (age 56) had died suddenly. He had been to his doctor on Friday morning and had been told he was fine. Three days later he was gone. I was very sorry I had not let Ed tell him we were expecting a baby.

What followed is all a blur. There is no preparation for early, sudden, death. I met most of my new relatives at the funeral home and service. I was a part of the family, yet still an outsider. Morning sickness had kicked in and I had more than a few awkward moments.

Three weeks later I had our first miscarriage. I began bleeding when Ed was at work and by the time he came home I knew it was over. When I told him what happened his first response was, "Dad has his first grandchild!" What he meant was, that our baby was in heaven with Bert. I truly believe this is true. We are Christians. We believe that God is true and real. That God sent his Son Jesus to earth so that through Jesus' death and resurrection we can have a relationship with God. That after death we will go to heaven. Bert believed this and so we can know he is with God.

Knowing that our baby was in heaven was small comfort to me. What had happened? Why had it happened? Why was my baby gone? The shock was very real, the questions many, and the loss painful.

It had never occurred to me that I would lose a baby. I had a plan for my life. I was going to grow up and be a wife and mother. I had no interest in a 'career.' I thought that there would be times when I would work outside the home but my focus would be my husband and children. What had just happened?

It's like my world had just been tilted on its axis. I lost my grounding, my foothold in life. We had our families and friends and so we had support but what did they know? In those early days I felt very alone. Ed was dealing with the loss of his Dad and I was dealing with the loss of our baby. We weren't much help to each other.

The day I lost our second baby was horrific. I had been feeling fine except for the morning sickness that had dogged me for the previous three weeks. I had gone for a walk and to meet a friend for coffee. On the way home the pain started and when I got in I realized I was bleeding. I called the doctor's office and spoke with the nurse. She called back to say the doctor didn't think there was any point in coming in today, come in a couple of days and see him. When I did go he confirmed that the baby was gone and suggested I go home, relax, and enjoy life. He said I was young and would probably have lots of babies! He obviously had no understanding of the loss. He was not unique in my experiences with doctors and medical personnel.

By the end of 1985, I'd had my third miscarriage. I was beginning to consider that it was possible that I would not have children of my own.

2. Unfit!

How does one accept that what you planned, longed for, and expected, may not happen? Having children of your own is a right, isn't it? . . . Maybe not! . . . As my world continued to spin off its axis I looked for a way to right it again. Friends and family offered advice and comments. I was given and I found, several books on childlessness. Most were unhelpful.

Everyone had a story about how their mother, aunt, cousin, or someone, had a number of miscarriages and then had a healthy child. Many people suggested we adopt a child and then we'd have a 'real' one of our own! These comments were not helpful! Neither were most of the books we read. The one book I would recommend, if it is still available, is *The Ache For A Child*, by Debra Bridwell. This one was very helpful in getting me adjusted to life with the possibility of no children.

There was an emptiness that I couldn't shake. A hollow place in and beneath my heart that I couldn't escape. It was like a physical ache that never went away.

By the late 80s we were living in Valleyfield, Prince Edward Island, so we applied to the Province of PEI to adopt a child or children. We did not ask for a 'healthy newborn.' We asked for a child or sibling group, under the age of six. We were accepted on the waiting list and told it could be at least a seven year wait and there were no guarantees.

The following year we applied to be foster parents. It is an interesting process to go through. A 'home study' is required of all foster and adoptive parents. Two social workers came to our home for a number of two to three hour visits. Every aspect of our life was exposed to scrutiny. I don't think there is really any other way to assess a couple but it sure is invasive. I wonder how many people would be parents if this process was required of everyone before they had a child.

As we were coming to the end of our assessment I asked the two social workers how we were doing. They responded that our next meeting was probably going to be the last. They couldn't see any reason why we wouldn't proceed and become foster parents.

Imagine my shock, horror, pain, and anger when they came back the next week and said they had a problem. They said someone had come to them and made some allegations against me. They'd been told that I was racist, that our marriage was falling apart, that I abused the residents at my job, and that Ed had told someone that I was mentally unstable! We were not told who had said this. (Years later we found out who and why. She is a very unhappy person and very bitter. I feel sorry for her.) There was really no way to fight the accusations. How do you fight a ghost? Since there was no way to proceed we withdrew our names for becoming foster parents.

Some months later I called to see where we were on the list for adoption and found out that we had been taken off that list. I was told by the Provincial Director for adoptions that since we'd had the allegations concerning fostering that she couldn't proceed with an application for adoption. I asked if we could fight the allegations and she said it was too late.

After we had been married seven years, and again after fourteen years, Ed asked if we could re-open this and have our names cleared but each time we were told no. We didn't think to go the legal route but looking back I am fairly certain that had we hired a lawyer, things could have been very different. It just didn't occur to us to do so at the time.

Shortly after my seventh miscarriage I had a follow-up appointment with my family doctor, Dr. Robert Colborne. After a few minutes of listening to me whine about not having children he became very angry. He slapped his hand on the desk and said in a loud voice, "That's enough! Give me ten things you are thankful for!"

I began to cry and in a wimpy voice replied, "But I don't have children."

He slapped the desk again and said, "Ten things. NOW!" When I hesitated he said, "I'll start for you. You have Ed. Well, he should count for two! You have your Mother. You have your Father and he is not a drunk! Now come on. Give me the rest!" He wouldn't let me leave the office until I had given him ten things I should be thankful for. As I left I realized from the looks on the faces of those in the waiting room that everyone had heard him!

A few days later I was just settling to sleep after working nights when I got a phone call. I answered it and this voice said, "Are you still being thankful? Give me ten things!" This was the last time he mentioned this but I knew that what Dr. Colborne was trying to do was to change my attitude. It did help me see things differently but he also seemed hard and cold.

Some months later Dr. Colborne was called to my place of work to see an elderly lady. After he was finished his call he asked for a word with me. He told me that earlier in the day he had been with a teenager as she delivered her baby. He said as he held the little boy he thought of Ed and I and wished he could give us this little one. I was quite touched. What kindness! On the one hand to be stern with me about changing my attitude and yet on the other to wish he could make it better. Dr. Colborne is gone now but I will never forget how he cared enough to challenge me. How he cared enough to want things to be different. He was someone I knew I could count on.

At one point in our journey we decided that enough was enough. I was 35 years old and we had been married for 13 years. We'd had ten miscarriages between six and fourteen weeks gestation. Each of these losses was very real to us. Each held the promise of a son or daughter to love, and nurture, and watch grow. Each held the promise of a grandchild, a niece or nephew, and a cousin. After a few losses I would try not to get my hopes up. One of the ways of doing this was to not talk about being pregnant to anyone. Then after the loss there was no support or understanding. If I did share then people would get excited with me—maybe this time I'd carry to term!

So we decided, as I said, that enough was enough. We made the decision that I would have a tubal ligation. This would end the dream of giving birth and it would provide some level of closure. I felt it would help me move on. We only shared our decision with four people. Two of them being our good friends who happened to be a doctor and wife couple. We were at their home for a meal and visit and we talked about our decision and how we had to come to it. I had to leave to go work but Ed stayed longer. It was after I left that they told Ed we were making the wrong decision. That we were giving up too soon. When I heard this I was *really* angry! Giving up too soon! What did they know! How many years and how many miscarriages and how much emotional pain would be enough for them! The really sad part of this is that Ed wavered. He thought we should reconsider. I didn't go through with the tubal ligation and we went on to have more losses and more pain.

In my late 30s we were strongly encouraged by Ed's new family doctor to investigate further the medical issues surrounding my losses. He said there had been many advances in the area of infertility and miscarriage. I was reluctant, not wanting to get our hopes up again, but I consented. We went to a clinic in Moncton. We enjoyed the doctor and staff very much. They were respectful, kind, and professional. Over a period of about seven months we went regularly to appointments for tests and follow-ups. Our PEI Medicare plan paid for the actual visits and tests but we paid all the expenses in getting there. It was a three hour drive each way. Sometimes I would need to be there at 6:45am, two days in a row. We spent a lot of money on hotels, gas, meals, and the bridge toll.

Our clinic trips came to an abrupt end. I was the victim of a sexual assault. It is not an experience that I want to talk about here but it did affect us. I had to let the clinic staff know what had happened. They sadly informed me that I would have to put everything on hold for six months. I needed to have a clear AIDS test before they would continue. It was extra heart ache on an already painful event. In the end I did get a clear AIDS test but I did not go back to the clinic.

After the assault I sought medical attention. The doctor I saw said I could call his clinic to set up a time for a pregnancy test. Getting the test was no problem but getting the results was not so easy. I called his clinic and his receptionist refused to let me talk to him, stating that I was not his patient. I explained that I had seen him in the hospital emergency and was calling as a follow-up to that. She insisted on knowing what it was about so I had to tell her. She put me on hold and after a few minutes the doctor picked up the phone. A couple of hours later one of my good friends called, all excited to find out the results of my pregnancy test! What had happened was that just as the receptionist was putting me on hold the doctor came out of his office to call another patient from the waiting room. She called out to him and said my full name and that I wanted the results of my pregnancy test. My friend and about a dozen other people heard the exchange from the waiting room seats a few feet away! This was an example of medical staff who did not consider my feelings when dealing with me and certainly did not respect my privacy.

So—here I am—I can't carry a baby of my own. I can't foster a child. I can't adopt a child. I felt unworthy and unfit. I carried that label of unfit for seventeen years. Every time I had anything to do with other people's children I told them that I was considered unfit for fostering or adoption. I wore the label of unfit as if it was a neon light flashing from my forehead. There was no escaping it or setting it aside—I was unfit!

During the time of my childlessness and being labeled unfit, all around me there were babies. Many of our families and friends were having children. There were many times that even though I was very happy for the new parents my eyes would leak. I avoided baby showers. One of the ways I coped was to write. Here is a verse from that time:

Empty Arms

There goes one peeking out of a stroller,
Another one sits on his father's shoulder.

All around me on every side,
Babies can be seen there's nowhere to hide.

My first was due in the summer of 85,
But my little baby did not survive.

The second and third, shared the same fate,
None of my babies made their due date.

My breasts ache so badly from wanting to feel,
The tug of my little ones having their meal.

The crib in the corner stands empty and clean,
It leaves a big hole inside of my being.

There's no one to teach about reading and play,
No one to take to Grandma's for the day.

I watch from the sidelines and see them go by,
I can't take them home and must just say hi.

For all the joys and blessing of life,
My arms remain empty into the night.

When a person is childless there are many losses. There is the loss of not carrying a child and being pregnant. There is the loss of never knowing what a child from you and your spouse will look, act and be like. There is the loss of not being able to parent and teach a child. There is the loss of the potential joy of being a grandparent. There is the loss of sharing in society as a fellow parent. There are other losses which may mean more to one person than another. For me, I really wanted to be nine months pregnant with my husband's child and go through the actual experience of giving birth. I wanted to breast feed a baby. For those who decide to have a child and a child comes these are issues they never have to face. Never have to face and often do not understand. Being allowed to adopt or foster would not have fulfilled all these needs or losses but it would have greatly helped with most.

3. The Childless Years

I would hate to leave the impression that my life was all pain or all black because this certainly wasn't true. Yes, I was childless. Yes, I ached for this to be different. But, life was still good. One of the things we decided to do was to be involved in the lives of children whenever we could. That meant helping with sporting groups, babysitting for family and friends, teaching Sunday School, and much more.

I remember once dropping by my sister's home and she was talking about the expense of footwear for her children. She allowed me to buy sneakers for her kids. Funny how this was a big deal for me, but think about it. I took a child in my car to the store and bought them a pair of sneakers! That was the kind of everyday, mundane experience that most people around me were doing but that I wasn't a part of.

For a couple of years in the late 80s we enjoyed many happy times with a family of four young children. They were between six and ten years old when we met them, three boys and a girl. How they came to be at our home and part of our lives is their story but the joy and fun of it is mine. We were living in a small two bedroom house and yet they often stayed overnight. They helped us garden, shoveled and played in snow, played board games, and generally had tons of fun. We went on several adventures to the beaches and Rainbow Valley. They loved to eat out. Ed read to them by the hour! They were polite, respectful, appreciative, interested and interesting, and just a joy to have around. It was very quiet after they moved out of our area. I missed them terribly.

There are two families in particular, that 'shared' their children with me. One was a family in Lennoxville, Quebec. I know this will sound crazy to many of you but one of the losses of not having children is that I didn't have the opportunity to cook for them. I wasn't part of the everyday activities of cooking, cleaning, laundry, etc. When I visited in Lennoxville, which I did often, this family accepted me as one of them. I was part of meal times, play times and work times! Being there always brought healing to my aching heart.

The other family live here in our community. For the last ten years of my being childless, this couple allowed me to be part of their children's lives. I knew the children from babies. They often visited, with or without their parents. What a blessing it was to be able to share in family life on a regular basis!

For about ten years Ed and I ran a children's program at our church that we called, Kids' Club. From fall to spring we'd meet every Friday evening for two hours. For the first couple of years we limited it to children in grades 3-6 but then changed it to K-7. I *sooooo* loved this time! The evening started with games, then we'd have snack and talk about our week, and then have a lesson.

We took the children on a yearly outing to a hotel with a pool. What fun! More than once it was the first time one or more of them had ever stayed in a hotel. I loved to hear the squeals of delight and laughter as they discovered that they had their own beds and each room had it's own bathroom! We would be in the pool at least twice and all came home looking like prunes. I think I enjoyed these overnights as much or more than the children.

We had our annual 'Snow Day.' At one Charlottetown school there is this wonderful, steep, dangerous hill that thousands of people have used for sledding and sliding. You know the kind of slope I mean—it scares the wits out of most parents! We would go down on crazy carpets, inner tubes, toboggans, and if it was really icy, on our bums. The screams and squeals could be heard several blocks away. After we were all dead tired and starving we would go to a restaurant for lunch. What fun these snow days were!

In the fall we would have what I called our 'Harvest Celebration.' The children would invite their families and we had games and lots of food. We would cover one table with a blank table cloth and everyone would sign their names in permanent marker. One year I decided that the church should smell and feel like fall so I asked the children to bring bags of leaves. We spread nine large bags of leaves over the carpeted floor! It smelled great but what a mess to clean up after about eighty people had walked on them for two hours!!!

Every May we would have a closing dinner where the children cooked for their parents. They planned the menu, decorated the church, cooked the meal, and served it. In June we would come out to Valleyfield and have a walk through the woods and a bonfire. During the summer we would keep in touch with a beach day. Kids' Club ran for ten years. Over 200 children participated for one or more years.

A number of the children from Kids' Club became part of our Sunday School program and we saw them more than just on Friday evenings. I was asked by numerous kids over the years why I didn't have children of my own. I just explained that my body didn't work and my babies didn't stay inside long enough to live.

One Sunday morning we were looking at the story of Hannah from the Old Testament. Hannah was childless and she had prayed for a baby for a number of years and finally God answered her with baby Samuel. One of the boys asked me if I believed God answered prayers and I said yes. He then wanted to know if I had prayed and asked God for a child and I replied yes. Well, where is your baby then, came the next words. I explained that God is not a puppet on a string. He does not give us everything we ask for. Sometimes God answers no. After this exchange one of the girls stated that she was very happy I did not have children. That stunned me and when I had checked my emotions I asked her why she felt that way. I will never forget her reply. She said I was the only person who loved her who didn't have to. Her parents loved her because she was theirs. The same for the rest of her family and the teachers at school at least liked her because it was their job to. She said I was the only person who loved her just for herself because I chose to. She said if I'd had children of my own I probably wouldn't love her!

One very special Friday evening happened when Ed was away. His mother was dying and he had gone to Ontario to say goodbye. When the children arrived they wanted to know where Ed was but I delayed telling them till everyone got there and I could let them all know at once. I explained where he was and why. There were lots of questions. Someone wanted to know if we should pray and ask God to make Mynie better. I told them that certainly they could ask God that but what Ed was asking God for was that his mother would have a peaceful death. Some of the kids were not sure about that idea. After some time of talking one of the little girls said we should pray. She bowed her head and said, "God please help Ed's Mommy and Daddy have a real good reunion, real soon. And please give Ed a hug because I'm too far away and he will be sad. Thanks. Amen." Out of the mouths of babes!

I could write pages on all the memories and joys of our time running Kids' Club & Sunday School. Alongside my pain and my grief from so many losses there was also much joy, pleasure, and happiness.

For a person who is childless there are a number of times throughout the year when the pain can be more acute than others. Holidays were often one of these times for me. Rather than stay at home and avoid them I took a different approach. I looked around our circle of family and friends and community to see who else might be feeling left out or alone, for whatever reason. I would invite them to share a meal with us and spend part of the holiday together. Over the years I've had wonderful times sharing meals around our table.

Along my journey I learned that some parents name their unborn children who have died. I really liked this idea. I hated the fact that just because my children were gone before they were born it was as if they didn't exist at all. The other cool thing we learned is that some families have a living memorial for their lost babies. With these things in mind we named two of our children. 'Jamie' came in April 2001 and we planted a red maple tree for him. 'Eliza' came in March 2006 and we planted a white lilac for her.

Ed really likes the name Eliza. I joked that with Eliza for a first name and Van Donkersgoed for a last name she would have half of the alphabet covered! I wrote a poem/song for both Jamie and Eliza. Here is Jamie's.

A Song for Jamie

You were just a little flutter
growing underneath my heart,
with you came so many hopes
and dreams about new life.
As each day passed and time went by
my love it grew and grew,
I longed to hold you little one
and see what you could do.

But there's
Empty arms and an empty crib,
no one to play ball with.
Empty arms and an aching heart,
no one to swing in the park.
Jamie, you're not here.

The day you died I was at work
planting flowers and shrubs,
Thinking of your own sweet Dad
and how you'd win his heart.

The pain it came and then I knew
you would not come to me,
I knew I would not hold you
nor sit you on my knee.

There's a maple growing on the lawn
it's standing tall for you
It tells the world I loved you
and that always will be true.
It's reaching up with out stretched arms
saying to everyone,
A marker for the world to know,
Jamie was my son.

I often sit and wonder
and think of you with God
wondering if you're missing me
and if you see my heart.
Oh, Jamie dear, I'll come to you
When this my life is gone
and then we'll have eternity
as mother and her son.

For there's
Empty arms and an empty crib,
no one to play ball with.
Empty arms and an aching heart,
no one to swing in the park,
Jamie's gone ahead.

Jamie's gone ahead.

4. Ellie

In July 2007 there was an ad in our local newspaper looking for foster parents in this area. It came at a time when I was struggling again with my age and the fact that it was very unlikely I was going to be a mother. Ed and I had been talking and praying about what to do. Would we try once more on the medical front? Would we try again to adopt? As we were sorting this out the ad appeared in the paper. We decided that we would answer the ad and leave it with God. If we were accepted, fine, we would go with that but if not then I knew that the time had come to put the idea of motherhood to rest.

Imagine our surprise when we received a positive response from Child & Family. We were sent a package of information and a self assessment form from Mary Walker*. She was one of the two workers who had assessed us all those years ago when we last applied to foster. We filled in the forms and proceeded with the application. In the initial review of our application, we fully discussed with Mary the impact of the false accusations from seventeen years earlier. She listened as I shared the pain and effect this had on my life. Then, she said we had been treated unfairly. My mind went wild! Here was an admission from someone from Child & Family that what had happened was wrong. It didn't change the years of pain. It didn't change my feelings of being found unfit, at least not right away. But it did begin the healing.

The whole process of assessment to see if we would make acceptable foster parents was long, invasive, and often uncomfortable. Ed and I are, in general, very open people so that did help. From our initial application in July of 2007 it took until August the following year before we had our first placement.

We signed a confidentiality agreement when we became foster parents and so there is much about this time that I cannot write about.

We had only been foster parents for a few months when we first heard about Ellie*. The social worker leading our foster parent's support group mentioned that she needed a home for a teenager who was expecting a baby. Right away I thought that this was something I could do, but I didn't say anything.

The next day I could not get Ellie out of my mind. I felt drawn to her. It's strange how strong the pull was because at that point I didn't even know her name. When Ed came home from work I asked how his day was. He said it was ok but he had thought about Ellie all day! We decided that I would call the social worker and ask if she would consider us for a foster home for Ellie.

The social worker was very concerned that I was interested because I wanted the baby. It really hadn't occurred to me. My thoughts were about how Ed and I had learned to cope with so much in our lives that maybe we could help this girl. Also that she would need time and that I was not working outside of the home at the moment. We had one other foster child at that time. After several meetings and discussions it was decided that Ellie would come to live with us. She visited a few times and then moved in.

We fell in love with Ellie. Again I can't share much about this time. I do remember the first time she laughed! I was sitting at the computer answering emails when I heard this sound coming from the kitchen - it grew louder and sort of bubbled over. I stopped to listen and heard Ellie and the other child laughing and teasing Ed about his hair (or lack of it) as they were doing the dishes. It is a precious memory.

Over the next few months Ellie became part of our home. She went to school. She learned to cook and clean. We played board games and cards. She became part of our circle of family and friends and Sunday Dinners. Except for the constant meetings with social workers and youth workers, we were like a family.

After a couple of months in our home Ellie started hinting that she would like to be adopted by us. I was thrilled with the idea but knew that it was not something we could discuss yet. A few weeks after Ellie had her baby it came up again and she mentioned it to her social worker. The worker called me and I let her know that Ed and I were open to this.

In the summer of 2009, I was called into a meeting with Child & Family and told that there had been a discussion about the long term plan for Ellie. They were willing to proceed with her adoption to Ed and I. What a thrill! We were told it was a lengthy process but that it would start within the next couple of months. There would be meetings with us and meetings with Ellie.

I wish I could share all that happened during this time. I will say that it was one of the happiest of my life. I couldn't have loved Ellie more if she was born to me. We were able to take Ellie with us on a trip to Quebec and Ontario. She rode on an elephant, drove through a pride of lions, and watched as baboons climbed all over our car at the African Lion Safari. She stayed with us at our friend's home in Lennoxville and participated in the festivities of their son's wedding. She learned to garden, swam in the pool, and hung out with her friends. Our home was a happy, busy place.

Some months went by and the promised meetings to proceed with Ellie's adoption did not happen. No one even scheduled a meeting or called Ed and I. Ellie had them scheduled and then cancelled. Ellie started to get frustrated and worry that the adoption wouldn't happen at all.

During this time Ellie's baby was living with us. In January 2010 Ellie was told she had to make a permanent plan for her baby. She began to ask if Ed and I would adopt her and the baby but her social worker told her she had to choose. She could not be adopted by us herself and give us her child to adopt at the same time. In the spring she decided she didn't want to be adopted and then decided that we could adopt her baby.

Ellie doesn't live with us now. We have told her she is always welcome and I hope and pray she knows this. She is a lovable, engaging young woman who has survived despite much turmoil in her early life. She bounces into our home for short visits, calling us Mudder and Fadder. I see her as my own and ache for more time with her. From the moment Child & Family agreed to allow us to adopt her I have felt like her mother and that isn't going to change. In my heart she is my girl!

5. Gracie

Gracie was born on April 11, 2009. I was there when she entered the world. A 6lb 12oz beautiful, baby girl! It had been a long night and day. I was exhausted and emotional. Here was this wonderful new little life. I'd had the privilege of sharing the journey of this courageous young woman as she gave birth to Gracie. As I watched Mom and baby I was reminded, yet again, that I was childless.

For most of Gracie's first three days I was at the hospital with her and her Mom. This was a precious time. The miracle of birth and new life never grows old!

At three days old Gracie came home to live with us as a foster child and so there is much of her early story I cannot tell. I will say that Gracie was a very happy, contented, and peaceful baby. She slept through the night by two months and smiled for everyone who looked at her!

Gracie was a foster child in our home for one year. At the end of that year her Mom left her with us as an alternate arrangement. For the next nine months, life was an emotional roller coaster. Her Mom wanted us to adopt Gracie but Child & Family were not in favor of this. She was strongly encouraged by her social worker to try and parent but was not encouraged to look at alternatives such as adoption. A lawyer who was provided to her to work on her behalf, strongly encouraged her to allow Gracie to be put with younger parents with more financial resources. It seemed to us that no one was taking into account that Gracie was attached to Ed and me. We had been her family since birth. With us she also had a secure world of extended family and community that she knew and cared about and who cared about her. Also, we would be willing and able to maintain an open adoption and relationship with the birth Mom. What a difficult time this was! Finally when Gracie was 21 months old her mother gave us guardianship of Gracie. This led to her adoption in August 2011.

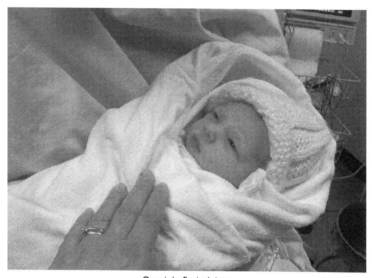
Gracie's first picture

Gracie's adoption was not arranged by Child & Family so it was a private adoption. This meant that we had to hire a lawyer who is a Licensed Adoption Agent. She facilitated all the legal requirements and assessments necessary to fulfill the law. From the time we were made Gracie's legal guardians to the final court date had to be a minimum of six months. I cannot describe to you the feeling of going to court and hearing the judge say I could be Gracie's Mom! After all the losses, and the years of being labeled unfit, and after the ups and downs of the first two years of Gracie's life I was now her MOM! I was no longer childless. I was 49 years old and had been married for 27½ years and I was finally, officially, a Mom!

Gracie's Court Day

In preparing Gracie for court I explained to her that we would go and see a judge and that he was going to tell us that Ed and I could be her Mom and Dad forever. We told her she would get a new name. We kept her first name but changed her second name to 'Ruth,' after her favorite aunt. Gracie referred to the judge as her 'forever judge,' and said he was, 'good'!

For weeks before the adoption Ed had been inviting our friends and family to an open house to celebrate. About 100 people came, including Gracie's birth mom! Most of those who came knew about my struggle with childlessness and my miscarriages, so it made for a very special celebration.

Gracie was very overwhelmed with all the people and the noise so she left the party to go and play in the mud puddles in our yard. A number of people came to me to report she was getting her special dress muddy but I didn't care. MY little girl was enjoying chasing a frog through the mud puddles in front of our home and we were both happy!

Gracie in the mud puddle on court day!

Gracie is a beautiful child inside and out. She has brought joy to many with her smile and chatter. She is secure in her world of family and friends. I so enjoy the way she views the church family as her own personal audience. She is growing up knowing the love of God and the love of family. What a great start in life!

6. Emma

How Emma came to us is a miracle. Her Mom, Lydia*, was part of our circle of family and friends. The first I heard about Emma was when Lydia was about five months pregnant. Lydia told us that she had been for an ultrasound at the IWK and that the doctors had told her that there was very little chance Emma would survive birth. Lydia was strongly encouraged to have an abortion. She refused and her pregnancy continued. I could not imagine being in Lydia's situation.

When Lydia was about 7½ months pregnant she was at our home for a gathering of family and friends. She sat in the big green arm chair, a little unsure of herself. Gracie, then about 16 months old, climbed up into her lap and snuggled down for a cuddle. They stayed like that for about an hour. It was as if Gracie knew that Lydia needed comfort. Ed feels that even then Gracie felt a connection to Lydia & Emma.

Emma arrived two weeks early, on September 20, 2010, at the IWK. She pinked up right away and breathed on her own. Lydia was able to hold her before Emma was taken to the PICU for assessment. I wasn't there during this time and only have second hand accounts of what happened. I have been told that Emma did far better than first expected. She had surgery on day eight and that went very well. Her official diagnosis is: Complex congenital heart disease, dextrocardia with AV septal defect, transposition of the great arteries, pulmonary atresia, total anomalous pulmonary venous drainage, and asplenia.

On October 4, I made the trip to Halifax to see Lydia and Emma. I was able to go into the NICU and hold Emma. She was beautiful! It was hard to absorb that she had such medical issues. I felt very drawn to her in a way that I can't really explain. I did not want to leave her and Lydia but I was only there for a one day trip.

When Emma was three weeks old she was transferred to the QEH. Shortly after, Emma was placed in the temporary care of Child & Family. When she was ready to leave hospital Emma was taken to a foster home. I would love to recount to you all that happened over the next few months but that isn't my story to tell. I will say that Lydia had done nothing to harm her child and no one accused her of doing so. She had only birthed her and loved her.

In early spring Lydia had to make a choice. She wanted so badly to bring Emma home and be her Mom but that wasn't to be. It was at this point that Ed and I started talking about adopting Emma. We offered an open adoption, where Lydia could maintain contact with Emma and Emma would grow up knowing that Lydia was her first Mom.

On April 6, 2011, Lydia and her partner proposed an alternate plan to Child & Family. This plan was for Ed and I to adopt Emma. We were thrilled to have another daughter but we ached for them as they were forced to make this decision. This is the fact of adoption—most often it means agonizing pain and loss on one side and unimaginable joy on the other. We were still working through Gracie's adoption when our lawyer took on Emma's case.

In April, Emma underwent a second heart surgery. Ed and I longed to be with her but we were denied this. In fact we were denied access to Emma until June. The social workers tried hard to dissuade us from proceeding with the adoption, even giving false financial information concerning her medical needs. Emma was often referred to as a 'medically fragile child' who could not be around other children. We met with her paediatrician and the information he gave us was different than what we were hearing from the foster parents and social workers. During this time Ed was very confident and steadfast in his faith that God would work out the details. I was not so sure and just wanted to get to know our new daughter.

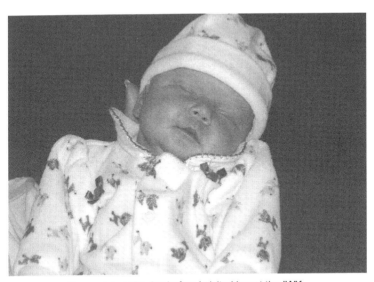

Emma, taken the day before I visited her at the IWK

Most of our family and friends were excited for us but a few thought this was a very bad idea. One factor was our age—that we were too old to be adopting children. While it is true that we were past the normal age range to parent, people are waiting longer to have children. We are mature enough to be able to cope with the issues surrounding open adoption. We are mature enough not to be threatened by the fact that our children will know and love their birth parents.

Another factor was Emma's health. More than one person asked why we would consider adopting a child who we know has a lower life expectancy than most. A child who has such huge medical issues. I don't have a clear answer. Our decision to parent her was not dependant on her health. She was going to face many health concerns and hospital visits and I just wanted to be there to love her through it all. I am well able to deal with unexpected medical upheavals and am a very flexible person. Her health was not a worry for me, just a learning curve I was willing to climb.

The other factor was money. We are not rich. We have made choices about work and lifestyle that have allowed us time for things we have felt are important but have not left us with a healthy bank account. Can being a parent really be about money? We had no idea, and still don't, what is ahead for us with Emma. We do know that God will provide what we need.

Emma's transition to our house finally happened in June. It was very difficult! Her foster Mom made it very clear to us that she did not approve of the plan and did not think we would take good care of Emma. Just imagine beginning to get to know your nine month old daughter with two social workers and the foster parents looking on! At one point we were told that we couldn't let Emma cry because it would cause brain damage. You should have seen the look on the paediatrician's face when we asked about this! As he tried to hold back the laughter he explained that children need to cry as part of their development and Emma was not at risk of brain damage from crying.

First Picture of Emma & Mommy

At the time of her placement with us Emma was being fed with a nasal gastric (NG) tube. She was eating very small amounts of cereals and other solids. When Emma was born she nursed and then drank from a bottle but since it took so much energy for her to suck, the NG tube was the best option. After her April surgery it was expected that she would not need the tube but she was still on it. Between five and seven hours a day were spent with her hooked up to a feeding pump. At the same time we were forging emotional attachments with Emma we were learning the ropes of tube feeding.

After about ten days of visiting with Emma every day we finally had her at our house with no supervision. What a great day it was! We took her across the road to meet my parents. We took pictures of her and Gracie outside. For the first time we relaxed and just enjoyed her.

Emma getting to know her new Daddy

Transitioning a child into your home is an amazing experience. After that first time on our own I was very reluctant to have her go back to the foster family but we had to wait a little longer. On June 29, Emma came home to stay and we were made her legal guardians!

At 5:30am on June 30th Ed and I stood by the crib of our second daughter! We had to get her up for her first feeding of the day but we waited a moment and just watched her sleep. As Ed bent to pick her up she opened her eyes and immediately smiled at him. From that moment on she was nicknamed, 'Smiley'!

We decided to give Emma a couple of weeks to settle in and then we would follow the medical advice we had been given and wean her off the feeding tube. On July 5, we took her to Halifax for a follow-up appointment at the IWK Heart Center. The staff there were very supportive of her coming off the NG tube and gave us some good advice/information. She was taking about 900ml of formula a day through the tube. The reason she was not very interested in a bottle was because she was never hungry. We were advised to cut down on her feedings and when she was hungry she would drink. Over a period of four days we reduced her to about 600ml a day. Then on the fourth day she picked up a bottle and drank 45ml, no problem! There was no looking back. She quickly switched to a bottle and began eating more solid foods. We left the tube in until we were sure but on August 12 the tube came out. How wonderful for her to be free of it!

Gracie was thrilled to have a sister. She read to her and shared her toys. She 'helped' look after her by bringing things and choosing Emma's clothes. They laughed a lot and 'talked' with each other. There was no jealousy on Gracie's part. Emma quickly became part of the family as if she had always been here.

On June 30, Lydia and her partner came to see Emma. They hadn't seen her in three months. What a privilege it was to sit back and watch them be with their child. Emma smiled and responded to them. She wasn't shy or reserved. I was full of emotions as I watched my new daughter with her first parents. I prayed God would continue to work out the details as we raised Emma, while maintaining her connection to Lydia.

It's still a work in progress but I truly believe that adopted children can only benefit from having love, care, and support from all their parents.

Family picture from July 2011

For Emma our home was very different than what she was used to. My parents and two of my siblings live across the road from us and she saw them every day. Less than a week after Emma arrived some friends from Quebec came to camp in our yard for a few days. This meant 13 new people for Emma to meet! Early in July she came with us to my nephew's wedding and wowed everyone with her ready smile. Over the summer she met many more family and friends. Emma loves people! She thrived on being part of our busy lives.

On August 1st Emma spiked a fever. We had been told that if this happened we were to take her right away to see the paediatrician. We called the Paediatric Unit of the QEH and were told to bring her in right away. I was beginning to get to know the staff as we had been in several times to have her feeding tube replaced. Emma was examined right away and tests were done to try to find out why she had a temp. As a precaution, she was put on extra antibiotics and kept at the hospital for four days. Nothing showed up in the tests and her temp went down and stayed down so we brought her home. This all had a very big upside to it—I got four uninterrupted days with my daughter! I stayed right there at the hospital with her and got to know her better. It was a precious time.

It was a wonderful summer! Emma was with us for the celebration of Gracie's adoption. Our close family and friends welcomed Emma with open hearts. We began to build what we pray will be life long relationships and connections as a family. God had worked out the details for me to become a mother for a second time!

7. Sarah Anne

When we agreed to Emma's adoption we knew that another baby was on her way. She was due the first of September. We spent a lot of time praying and considering whether or not to adopt her as well. Certainly there was benefit for the baby to be raised with her sister. It would be easier for the birth parents to deal with one adoptive home instead of two. We definitely wanted more children. But did it make sense? We did need to consider our age, Emma's health, and how another baby would affect Gracie. After learning from the ultrasound that the baby was healthy and didn't have any of the health concerns that Emma had, we agreed to take her as well.

I became very excited. This would be very different than Gracie and Emma coming to our family. With Gracie I was there when she was born and she lived with us from birth but she was not mine. I held myself back from Gracie for more than a year, always reminding myself that I was not her mother. Emma did not come to us until she was nine months old and so we missed out on the first part of her life. Both girls were named before they were ours. With this new baby things were very different. She would be ours from birth. Not that the depth of our love could be any greater than it was for the other two!

I have always loved the name Sarah. I have a niece called Sarah and I asked her permission to call our baby, Sarah. She was delighted and immediately said yes. We added my name to get 'Sarah Anne.' I have a close friend with a daughter called 'Sarah Anne' and she too agreed for me to use the name again. Naming a child is something people do everyday but for someone like me who was childless for so long it was a very special moment.

I was with Lydia through most of her last few months of her pregnancy. We laughed together, we cried together, went to appointments, and talked. It was understandable then that I would be there for support the day the baby came. What a privilege! Sarah was born on August 18. It was, without a doubt, both the most amazing day and the worst day of my life. Lydia chose not to see Sarah right away. I left the delivery room with my new baby daughter cradled in my arms, to the sound of sobs from Lydia. A perfect picture of the utter joy, and utter pain, of adoption.

One of the losses of not being able to birth my own children was the experience of breast feeding. This is something I had really wanted to do. I was aware that adoptive moms could stimulate breast milk and I did some research into this. About 25% of women who try, get no milk at all. About 50 % get some milk. About 25% have enough milk to fully feed their baby. I began working on this in mid-April in hope that I would be able to nurse Emma. We had to wait until the end of June for her to come home and by then she was nine months old and had just got two teeth. I didn't have the courage to try nursing her! I did give her my breast milk through her NG tube and later in a bottle.

I was able to nurse Sarah Anne right away. I did need to supplement with formula for a while but by the time she was four weeks old I was able to fully feed her by nursing. What a thrill and joy this was! At 49 years old, married for over 27 years, I was mother to three little girls and I was nursing one of them! Gracie 27 months, Emma 11 months, and Sarah a newborn. God is full of surprises!

Sarah came home at two days old. Our lawyer had wrapped up Gracie's case six days before and now we added Sarah's! With a few minutes of our lawyer's time and some signatures, the hospital let us leave with our beautiful baby girl! Gracie wanted to hold her, help change her, feed her, and read to her. Emma just smiled, laughed, and pointed at her. It was a wonderful, busy, and happy time. I found myself waiting for someone to come and say they'd made a mistake and the girls couldn't stay! I think this is common with adoptive parents. With help from some family members and friends we fell into a routine of feedings, diapers, play, and sleep. Life was good!

When you adopt a child there are a number of different legal steps. With Sarah we were made her legal guardians the day we brought her home from the hospital but the birth parents still had a period of time to change their minds. It was only after they had signed away their rights to her and time was up for things to change that we sent out a birth announcement. Here is the email and some of the photos we sent to our family and friends on September 24/11 with the heading, 'And Baby Makes Three!':

Hello all,
   Some of you have been asking for pictures and an update of our girls and I think maybe a few of you don't know what's up.

I was waiting for some legal things to be firmed up before I sent pictures (Emma's & Sarah's adoption will be final in February but we are legal guardians to them both now).

Gracie (2 1/2) and Emma (12 months), were joined by "Sarah" Anne on August 18th. I was there when she was born and brought her home at two days old. We are all doing great and really enjoying our new busy lives!

First Family Picture!

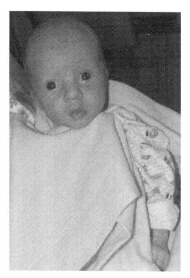

Sarah Anne
at three weeks

Gracie on the
walking trail

Emma's first birthday
(no need for a feeding tube now!!)

Let me say here how much respect I have for our birth moms. They have given me something that is so precious. So priceless. So totally amazing. I can never properly say thank-you because I don't know how. What are the words that describe having a baby come into my empty arms? Not just into my empty arms but into my empty arms forever. These amazing young women gave me part of themselves. They have trusted me to be their babies Mommy. I pray that I will be the kind of Mommy God wants me to be. I pray that He will guide my steps each and everyday.

8. September 27

September 27 was a wonderful, sunny, fall day. My parents were headed to a cottage in Chepstow for a few days by the ocean. Since Dad finds it tiring to drive that far we made a plan. I would drive him and Mom to the cottage in their car. I would get them all set up and then Ed would come and pick me up. Five and half week old Sarah came with me.

We were on the road by about 9:00 am. Mum had done a good job of carefully packing everything they would need for their three day stay. Over the years they've had many short trips away and she has become expert at packing just the right things. It took almost an hour to reach the cottage. The scenery was beautiful, many places looking just as fresh as if it was spring.

We had only seen pictures of the cottage but it did not disappoint. It is right on the cliff overlooking the ocean. Inside is well kept and comfortable. It has the feel of a welcoming old friend who is glad to see us. Mum and Dad looked around and chose their room. On Thursday Ed and I were to come back with the children for an overnight. There was plenty of room and I was looking forward to it.

After helping carry in the supplies and luggage and getting things settled I sat down to nurse Sarah. She was a little quieter than usual. She nursed well and seemed to be satisfied. We made a nest for her with blankets on the floor and put her down for a nap. Mum and I discussed whether or not Sarah was ok. The past three days she had been sleeping longer between feeds, her stool was watery, and her abdomen seemed a slight bit larger. We thought she was fine but Mum suggested that I take her to the doctor, just to be sure.

September 27, taken on the beach at Chepstow, PEI

Ed arrived with Gracie and Emma and we had coffee together. After, Ed and I took the kids down onto the beach. Gracie found an alligator made out of red clay and sand. It was about six feet long and very well sculpted. The artist had made it near the high water mark so it was not affected by the tides. We took a few pictures, gave my folks a hug, said good-bye, and headed for home.

As soon as we got home I called the doctor's office to see if I could take Sarah in. The nurse didn't think the doctor had time to see us but said if we came at 2:00 pm she would have a look and maybe the doctor could spare a few minutes. I had about an hour so I took the time to make another batch of spaghetti sauce. I love doing this! It's a great way to use the tomatoes, onions, peppers, and summer squash from our garden.

Meanwhile, Ed had arranged to take our dog, Moses, to the vet. Moses was unwell and we had decided that it was time to have him put down. It was not an easy decision but we felt we had to as responsible pet owners. We tried to explain to Gracie that Moses was going to the dog doctor and that he would give him a needle and that Moses would not wake up again. That Moses would be dead. Gracie cried and did not understand. We did not expect her to.

Just before 2:00 pm Ed left with Moses for the vet. Emma was sleeping so I left her at home with a friend. I took Sarah and Gracie and headed for the doctor's office.

Karen, the nurse, took us in almost right away. She talked to me about Sarah and examined her. She left the room, saying she would be right back. A few moments later she returned with Dr. Jocelyn Peterson, a female resident who was working with Dr. Scott Campbell. She too examined Sarah and asked a few questions and then turned to Karen and said, "Which room is the doctor in, we need him *now*." I was a little surprised by her tone.

Dr Campbell came in moments later and asked questions as he examined Sarah. It had been twelve days since our last visit and at that time he had pronounced her perfect! He was all serious when he turned to me and explained that Sarah did have a problem with her abdomen. He was not sure what it was but said it would require us seeing a paediatrician and he was going to call one right away. He said he wasn't sure if I should take Sarah myself or go EMS. He left the room and I began to get a sense of unease in the pit of my stomach.

A few minutes later Dr. Campbell was back with instructions for me to go to KCMH, across the parking lot. He said Sarah was to have an x-ray, get an IV started, and have an NG tube inserted. He said he would send word to me there after he had spoken with the paediatrician.

I left the office bewildered. What just happened! I had come to the doctor's office to have them tell me my baby was fine and that I was just being a typically over anxious new mother. On my way to the hospital I remembered the spaghetti sauce simmering on the stove—I had planned on returning home right away! I called Ed on the cell. He was very emotional, having just watched Moses die. I told him what I knew so far and he came and got Gracie. I told him I would let him know what was happening as soon as I knew.

At the hospital there was no wait. We went straight into x-ray and when we came out EMS were waiting for us. The resident who had been at the doctor's office was there. She said the paediatrician, Dr. Kathryn Morrison, was waiting for us at the QEH. The emergency room staff tried several times to get an IV started and couldn't. It was decided that we would go straight to Charlottetown. I was strapped onto the stretcher so I could hold my baby, loaded in to the ambulance, and we were off.

Sarah did not cry. She just lay there half asleep. A short time into the ride the paramedic asked about Sarah's blood sugar. He had no record of it being checked so he checked it. It was three. He was very concerned and after a discussion with his partner and a conversation with someone at the QEH he put the lights on and we sped the rest of the way. (Every time I hear the EMS siren tears come to my eyes as I remember that trip.)

When we arrived at the QEH there was no waiting. We went straight to Unit Five. I knew many of the staff from my visits with Emma. They immediately started an IV, inserted an NG tube, and drew blood for testing. As soon as Sarah was hooked up she was taken for an abdominal ultrasound. No one was saying much, including me. I was calm, just trying to take in what was happening. I knew we were looking at something serious when Dr. Morrison accompanied us for the ultrasound. As it was being done Dr. Morrison told me that Sarah may need surgery and if that was the case it would have to be done at the IWK.

I was having a hard time getting my head around the fact that a few hours earlier I had been sitting by the ocean, nursing my baby, and visiting with my parents. What was happening? It was three days ago that I sent out a happy notice to all our family and friends, announcing Sarah's arrival in our home!

I was watching Sarah deteriorate before my eyes. Her abdomen grew several centimeters over the course of the afternoon. I didn't leave her side. I was there for all the procedures, staying out of the way but doing what I could to help hold and to comfort. I was helpless, calm, and stunned by the turn of events. You cannot plan for emergencies of this kind. One thing that kept me calm was the attitude and manner of Dr. Morrison. We were dealing with something serious, that was obvious to all, but her calmness and control were a huge comfort to me. Her attitude and manner helped me keep my fear in check.

Somewhere around suppertime Dr. Morrison told me that Sarah would be airlifted to the IWK that evening. I would not be able to travel with her because every pound counts and they only carry the fuel they need for the patient, equipment, and staff. (I later learned that they also worry about the emotional state of the parents in the air!) I called Ed and he packed me some clothes and came in with Gracie.

Gracie was worried about Sarah and worried about me. We tried to explain that Sarah was sick and I would have to stay with her but Gracie was very weepy. Ed and I tried to figure out how I was going to get to Halifax. I called the airline but it was too late for the last flight. There was no shuttle until morning. We went outside Unit Five to the common area to talk and make phone calls. While we were sitting there our friend David Filsinger, Pastor of the Sherwood Church of the Nazarene, came by. He stopped to talk and stayed to pray. He knows our story of childlessness and heard that we had adopted two children but not about Sarah. It was comforting to see a familiar face and to have him pray with us.

We called a few family members and were trying to sort out what to do when Ed called our good friends Steve and Cindy to ask them to pray. Right away Cindy offered to drive me to Halifax. I asked about work and she said she was off for a few days. I didn't question this but just accepted it. We decided that Ed would go home with Gracie and I would wait for Cindy.

The air ambulance crew arrived at about 8:45 pm. They would need some time to get ready so we decided that Cindy and I would leave right away. It would take us longer to drive to Halifax than for them to fly. As I got ready to leave I was struck by the looks on the faces of the staff. There was no doubt that everyone was concerned about my baby. I didn't know what was coming but I knew it wasn't good. There are many moments that I will not forget—one of them is leaving Sarah for the flight crew to take care of while I drove the four hours to Halifax.

What can you say about a friend like Cindy? She dropped everything to drive me 350km, in the late evening, to a hospital, and the unknown of a sick baby. I learned that she had taken the time off work with the idea that another friend might need her support. It turned out that the other person did not need her at that time so she was free to come with me. One of the many details God had worked out!

9. PICU & Cancer

Cindy and I arrived at the IWK about 1:00 am. We were shown to an examining room in the emergency department where we found Sarah lying on a stretcher. She looked so tiny! I couldn't wrap my head around the fact that this was my little baby and we were here. I don't remember how long we were in the emergency unit before we were moved upstairs. No one seemed to know what was wrong, only that Sarah was very sick. The decision was made to move her to the PICU (Paediatric Intensive Care Unit).

The staff in the PICU were calm, kind, and comforting. They assured us that they would take good care of Sarah and suggested we get some sleep. There are several rooms just outside the PICU that are used by parents of their patients. We were given keys to the 'Condo.' It was a good size room with a double bed, lazy boy, TV, counter, closet, dresser, and it's own bathroom with a shower. I later learned that this was the largest and by far the nicest of these rooms. I went to bed exhausted but I'm not sure I slept much.

The following morning I learned that Sarah was to be seen by a number of specialists. One of the advantages of being in a hospital like the IWK, and in particular the intensive care unit, is that specialists can be called in for consultations, as needed. I was asked by a number of people to repeat the story of why I took her to the doctor the day before, what she was eating, her routine, and her history. For her part she fussed a little but mostly just lay there, her abdomen getting larger.

I'm not sure what time Cindy left but I do know that I encouraged her to go. It was wonderful that she had brought me over and supported me and looked after me. I assured her that if I needed her I would call. With a hug and a prayer she was gone.

At noon Sarah saw a Cardiologist. He checked her over and ran some tests and said her problems were nothing to do with her heart. At the time of his visit Sarah was quiet and actually looked pretty good. He asked why she was here. I started again to explain what had brought me to the doctor but he cut me off. He said no, not to the hospital but why is she in the PICU. He thought she was not sick enough to tie up a PICU bed. I had no answer.

This was Wednesday, September 28. In the afternoon I held Sarah for a few minutes. She fussed and didn't seem comfortable so the nurse suggested I put her back to bed. I didn't know it then but it would be three weeks before I held her again!

The day continued with consultations for Sarah and questions for me. I was learning the ways of the PICU. The team includes the staff intensivist (ICU doctor), registered nurse, respiratory therapist, ICU resident doctor, physiotherapist, dietitian, ward clerk, pharmacist, social worker and manager, as well as other health care team members. The staff intensivist on service when I arrived was Dr. Sherry Litz. Because the IWK is a teaching hospital there were numerous students around in a number of disciplines. I was told that I was welcome to be there for rounds and if I had any questions to ask the resident.

Sarah was deteriorating before our eyes. Her abdomen was continuing to grow. Her breathing was becoming more labored and she needed oxygen. A resident explained to me that this was because her swollen liver was pushing up on her lungs. No one knew why her liver was enlarged.

I spoke on the phone with Ed and my parents. Everyone had questions but there were no answers.

I didn't want to go to bed that evening but knew it was the sensible thing to do. The nurses promised to call if anything changed. Some time during the night I was awakened, though probably not really asleep, by an announcement for Dr. Litz to come to the PICU right away. My feet hit the floor and I was off running. I think she and I got there about the same time. Someone, maybe a nurse, was standing beside Sarah using a sort of bag to pump air into her lungs. The Respiratory Therapist wanted to intubate her. Dr. Litz said absolutely not. She said if Sarah was intubated she would die. There was a heated discussion but the doctor won out. Sarah was stabilized. The fact that I was tired and it was the middle of the night made everything seem worse. I felt very alone as I went back to bed. Dr. Litz assured me she would stay with Sarah and call if there was a change.

Thursday morning brought more tests and more questions. I was feeling calm and somehow peaceful but also feeling helpless. There didn't seem much I could do. I had not nursed Sarah since Tuesday morning. She was only getting IV fluids. I was given a pump and was expressing breast milk and freezing it. My supply was quickly decreasing, certainly due to the stress of the situation and the fact that I was not even able to hold Sarah. I decided to continue pumping so at least I would feel I was doing something to help.

It was Thursday afternoon that some answers started to come. Dr. Litz told me that she thought Sarah most likely had cancer. She said if I consented to the tests then they could confirm it. Cancer. One little six letter word that had such an impact. Cancer. My baby has cancer. After hearing the news I left the unit to catch my breath and get some perspective.

I was calm on the outside but inside I was raging at God. I shoved through the double doors of the unit and headed for the elevators. In my head I was railing at God. I was saying why? Why Sarah? Why was I alone? Why was I here by myself with not a soul who knew me? I continued this rant in my head as I entered the elevator and started down. I told God he was just going to have to work it out because I didn't know a single person in all this big hospital!

As I exited the elevator on the main floor I almost ran right into someone. I looked up to see Kay Gillis, a woman from my hometown. I had known Kay for years. She had given me my first real job. I stopped short and we both asked at the same time what each other was doing here. She told me and then asked why I was here. I told her about Sarah and my eyes started to leak again. She said I needed a mother's hug and pulled me into her arms saying that my Mom was not there so she would have to do. I knew instantly that she was God's answer to the rant in my head a few moments earlier. God already had her there waiting to comfort me. We spoke for a few minutes and then she left. Those moments meant so much to me. I never got a chance to tell her though or thank her. She died suddenly a couple of weeks later.

Thursday was the day I met Dr. Peggy Yap and Annette. Dr. Yap is the oncologist. Annette is the nurse assigned to walk us through the world of cancer. They explained that they needed to do a liver biopsy and a bone marrow biopsy. I agreed to both. It was from Dr. Yap that I first heard the name of the cancer: stage 4S neuroblastoma. Not a very common cancer but very treatable and curable in babies under one year. Dr. Yap asked if I would consider participating in a research project. I thought it very strange that she would be asking me at this particular time but she explained it. When the biopsy's were being done, extra tissue samples would be taken for the research. I agreed. I knew that the only reason the staff could know how to treat Sarah was because a parent before me had agreed to research.

I really didn't want to be by myself but I didn't know what to do. When I was talking with Ed on the phone he mentioned my nephew Evan, and reminded me he was in Halifax. He was a student at Dalhousie University and living close to the hospital. I called and Evan came to meet me. We ended up going to Smitty's for supper. He was good company and I so appreciated him taking the time to hang out. Even being at Smitty's was comforting as it was familiar to me and the coffee tasted the same as at the Smitty's at home!

I hadn't told Ed yet. I didn't know how to tell him over the phone. He was at home with Gracie and Emma. He was dealing with two little girls who were missing their Mom. He was answering the phone and emails and trying to hold everything together. He had decided that he would come over with my sister, and the girls, for an overnight. I would tell him then. Just before bed I changed my mind and called him. He learned over the phone that his six week old daughter had cancer.

I called Cindy and told her. She was not surprised. Cancer had not crossed my mind for one moment. As an oncology nurse it had already crossed hers. She prayed with me over the phone. Next I called my parents. They too, had already considered that it may be cancer. What else could it be?

On Friday Sarah was worse. She whimpered a lot and I was helpless to comfort her. Her abdomen had grown to 51 cm. Arrangements were being made for her to start chemotherapy the next day. She was moved from bed four to bed six. Bed four is out in the open with very little privacy. Bed six is tucked away in the corner with a sliding glass door. One of the nurses said Sarah was moved because she was so critically ill and might not survive. They wanted to give me privacy.

Ed and the girls arrived just after noon. It was so good to see them. The girls stayed with Ruth in the Condo while Ed and I spent some time with Sarah. It was hard as Gracie wouldn't let me out of her sight and Emma wouldn't come anywhere near me!

Ed spent a few minutes alone with Sarah and then we went off to the hotel to get them settled. It was so good to see them again and have Ed and Ruth to talk to about what was going on.

Saturday morning, Oct 1st, was Ruth's birthday. I had found her a present in the hospital gift shop for the girls to give her. It seemed such a normal thing to do in such abnormal circumstances! We went in to see Sarah and spent a few minutes with her. She seemed stable. The nurses told us they were getting ready to start her chemotherapy.

We took the girls in to see Sarah. Emma just pointed at her and laughed—just as she had done ever since we had brought Sarah home from the hospital as a newborn. Gracie was very serious. She wanted to touch Sarah and we lifted her so she could. We found her a stool so she could stand by the bed and see Sarah. After a few minutes Gracie started to sing *Jesus Loves Me*. When she was finished she said, "I sang to her, that will feel her better." My eyes were leaking again. Gracie asked if I needed her to sing to me. "I feel you better too, Mom!"

We left the hospital with the intention of spending time together and giving Gracie & Emma a little normalcy. We decided on the Halifax Farmer's Market. We often go the Charlottetown Farmer's Market so we thought this would be something familiar for the girls. Emma still would not come to me so Ed carried her. Gracie was sticking close to Ruth and so they went off together.

As Ed and I were wandering around we stopped to look at flowers. The woman beside us said to Ed, "I see you have your granddaughter with you." Ed laughed and told her no, it was his daughter and they chatted for a few minutes. As they spoke Ed mentioned Sarah and became emotional. We moved on to look at other things. A few minutes later the woman came up with a beautiful bouquet of flowers and handed them to Ed. She said she and her family wanted us to know that they cared and that they would pray. Our eyes started to leak. They couldn't know it but Ed really loves flowers. It meant so much to him!

I'd had enough wandering so I found a corner to sit. The woman next to me struck up a conversation. She said she was from BC and was visiting the Maritimes for the first time. As we talked she mentioned that her friends were taking her somewhere very special that afternoon but she couldn't remember where it was. I suggested Peggy's Cove and a few other places but nothing jogged her memory. As we were talking Ed came up with Emma and I introduced them. We spoke of Sarah and then Ruth showed up with Gracie. As we were talking I got a call on my cell from the hospital. We needed to return right away. I'm not sure I even said good-bye as we hurried off.

When we returned to the hospital we left the girls with Ruth while Ed and I went to the PICU. Sarah was much worse. Her abdomen had grown to 53cm. Her breathing was very labored. Dr. Litz was there and an Oncologist. They explained that if the tumor did not stop growing and start to shrink then Sarah would not live. Her body could not handle the pressure the tumor was creating. They felt the only hope was to do radiation and asked would we consent to it. After a short discussion we did, knowing that there were several big obstacles.

First, radiation is not done at the IWK. Sarah would have to go by ambulance to the hospital down the street. Moving her even a slight amount caused her to stop breathing so getting her there would be a huge risk. Second, radiation is not done on the week-end and this was a Saturday. Staff were not on-call or scheduled to work. They would have to be found to come in and open the building and start up the equipment. Third, she needed a CT Scan so it could be determined exactly where the radiation was to go. The CT Scan normally requires sedation in someone of her age and she could not be sedated.

We decided that Ed would go home to PEI with Ruth and the girls. We needed to think about Gracie and Emma and remove them from this situation. Ed did not want to leave me alone. He called Steve on his cell phone to see if Cindy would be able to come over again and stay with me. When Steve answered the cell phone he was sitting with Cindy at my parents home in Valleyfield! Cindy said she could come but she didn't have a vehicle. My Dad immediately handed over the keys to his car and asked her to go and look after his girls for him.

It took a couple of hours to get everything ready and then the EMS arrived to take us to the other hospital. I was told there was a good chance Sarah would not survive the trip so I brought her special blanket with me. Something to wrap her in and hold her as she passed.

In the back of the ambulance were Dr. Litz, a respiratory therapist, a nurse, and me. Dr. Litz insisted I stay close to my baby and I really appreciated that. Later the paramedic told me that in his six years on the job he had never traveled with such a team!

We arrived fine and the staff prepared for the CT Scan. Dr. Litz assured them that Sarah couldn't have any sedation but that she could immobilize her with padding and tape. Using pillows, bean bags, rolled up towels, and masking tape she was able to immobilize Sarah. She also gave her 'toot sweet,' a sugary liquid that acts as a pain killer for very small babies. Everyone was astounded by how quickly and well the scan went. There is a video feed from the radiation room so we all crowded around a small monitor screen to watch her as she was getting her radiation. Sarah was so well positioned her whole spine, one complete hip and most of the other hip missed the radiation! The plan was for Sarah to stay in the same position and not move her over the next few days. I was concerned about pressure sores but moving and turning her was not an option. She made it back to the PICU and all were very relieved.

What I didn't know until later was that at about the time we were moving Sarah, Ed was arriving at the ferry to go home to PEI. One of the first people he saw on the ferry was the woman I had been talking to at the Farmer's Market. She wanted to know about Sarah. As Ed was about to tell her she called her husband and friends over to listen. When he had told them she asked her husband, would you like to pray or shall I. The group immediately started praying for Sarah. They were on the ferry praying when we were moving to the other hospital and doing the radiation. Another sign of God's leading and sovereignty.

Cindy arrived late in the afternoon. I was very glad she was there. I didn't like Sarah being 'alone' and yet I needed sleep. Cindy slept in the chair by Sarah's bed for the next four nights. Not very pleasant for her but very comforting for me.

On Sunday, when we were getting ready to leave for radiation there was an argument between the paramedics and Dr. Litz. The paramedics wanted to put Sarah in a harness to transport her. This would require moving her and even a slight movement was causing her to stop breathing. She hadn't even been turned over in 48 hours. On the first trip for radiation we carefully picked up her mattress and put it on the stretcher, and belted the ends of the mattress down. The paramedics refused to do this saying their rules didn't allow it. Dr. Litz said Sarah would die if they repositioned her and the paramedics still refused to transport without Sarah being in a harness. Dr. Litz stood her ground and the paramedics called their supervisor. After a short conversation Dr. Litz got on the phone. I don't know what they were saying at the other end but she kept saying, "So you want this baby to die!" In the end she won out. Sarah was lifted on her mattress just as she had been the day before. The only difference this time was that Sunday's nurse would not let me help or travel with Sarah. The nurse was very rude and actually pushed me away. It was the first time I had not been allowed to help and participate in Sarah's care. Cindy and I ended up walking to the other hospital. It was a short walk physically but a long one emotionally as I wondered if Sarah had survived the trip!

As I was waiting for Sarah's treatment I overheard the staff talking about the woman who had done the CT Scan the day before. She had missed a very special event to help Sarah. I was stunned. The thought had crossed my mind that she had a very nice hair do. I hadn't thought to ask why. She had been friendly, efficient, and professional. I had no indication that she wanted to be anywhere other than where she was. She gave up something very special to willingly, and cheerfully, help my baby. For that I will always be grateful and thankful.

Monday's radiation trip was very different. On the week-end we were the only ones in the building. Everywhere was empty and eerily quiet. On Monday there were dozens of people around. Staff, patients, and families. It was crowded and noisy. It was also very sad as I realized all these people were on the same journey we had just begun. As on the other two days Dr. Litz, a nurse, and a respiratory therapist traveled with Sarah and the paramedics.

I'm not sure what day it was but early in that first full week I got an interesting perspective on Sarah's condition. One of the Specialists had been checking into the area of metabolic diseases. We had spent an hour together the first day Sarah was in the PICU as I tried to give her what I could of Sarah's family history. So here I was, a week later, walking down the hall in the hospital and I saw this doctor coming toward me. Her face lit up and she said, "You're Sarah's Mom, aren't you?" I replied yes and she gave me a quick hug as she said, "Oh, I'm so happy for you! I heard it was cancer! I am so happy for you!" She must have seen the stunned look on my face because she then said more quietly, "If you had needed my services it would have been palliative care. There would have been nothing I could have done to save your baby. With cancer, she has a chance." We spoke for a few moments longer and then I went off to dry my eyes. This put things in a different perspective.

10. The Journey Home

Beginning on October 5th I started to communicate with family and friends through email updates. The emails tell the story of Sarah.

DATE: WED, 5 OCT 2011 19:59

Hello all,

This is a hard note to write. Some of you know some details, some others, so I am trying to use one email to cover the information gaps. On August 18th, Ed & I were thrilled to welcome our third daughter, Sarah Anne. I was at the hospital with her birth Mom when Sarah was born and cared for her at QEH for two days before bringing her home on the 20th. We had a great five weeks together—Gracie & Emma love their new sister and we were settling into a great schedule of feeding, diapers, and chaos!

On Tuesday September 27th I took Sarah to our family doctor because she had a slightly swollen stomach and was just a little too sleepy and I was concerned about her. I expected to have the doc say she was fine. He was very concerned and sent us to the QEH and a few hours later Sarah was airlifted to the IWK in Halifax. Her abdomen grew very fast and by Friday September 30th we knew she had STAGE 4S NEUROBLASTOMA cancer. This is a very treatable cancer with an over 90% curable rate. It is fast growing but responds fast to treatment. The problem in our case is that even though we started chemotherapy first thing Sat morning Sarah was having trouble breathing because the growth was not leaving her any room for her lungs to move. Our only option was radiation. We consented to this and it was done on Sat, Sun, and Mon. The tumor stopped growing. Last night Sarah was getting so tired of working at breathing she was intubated. The thought is that by giving her a rest while the tumor shrinks we can buy her some time. Docs are all cautiously optimistic that she will make a full recovery. We just need her to hang on for a few more days. We are doing everything reasonable to help her, but not everything technically possible, and following docs advice. She is getting excellent care. If she pulls through the next few days and stabilizes it is quite possible that she and I will be here until Christmas while she receives further chemotherapy. Nothing is certain yet. I am staying in Halifax with Sarah at the IWK. Ed is home looking after Emma and Gracie. I will try to update every couple of days and you can contact me at this email and Ed at home at our usual email. I am peaceful in the midst of this. I know many of you are praying and regardless of the outcome we know God is good. Anne

As you can well imagine, I had many responses to this email. We have a large circle of family and friends who care about us. Ed had offers of babysitting, help with laundry, and meals. Our friend Ethel came to see Ed and asked if she could put the word out for donations to help us or could she organize a benefit concert. We were very blessed and encouraged with everyone's support.

Hello all,

Thank-you all so much for praying, helping, and caring. We are certainly feeling loved by you all! Sarah is holding her own. She is still needing assistance to breathe but is doing some of the work on her own. Over the past day she has been able to shed about a liter of fluid so as a result her girth has gone from a high of 53 cm to 46cm, today. The tumor is shrinking and the liver is slightly smaller. All this of course is very good. When the main Doc left yesterday he said if Sarah lived the week-end she had a good chance of making a full recovery. She is sooo tiny and I would love to hold her but that is not possible for a while yet.

Mum & Chris were over for a few hours yesterday. I know Mum was relieved to see Sarah for herself. Ed & Gracie came over today, with our friend Andrea. It was so good to see them all. I'm still trying to wrap my head around the fact that we are here and this is happening. It remains true that I am peaceful—a miracle really. If anything changes I will write sooner, otherwise I will write again in a few days.

Love to all,

Anne

This was the week Emma was supposed to be coming to the IWK for a sedated echocardiogram. It was a follow-up from her surgery in April. I knew that it was not something we could cope with as a family so I dropped by the IWK Heart Center to let them know. The Heart Center and the PICU are on the same floor, just down the hall from each other. The staff were really understanding and said they would get back in touch with me to re-schedule. About an hour later I was by myself with Sarah when a cardiologist walked in. I recognized him from our July visit with Emma but I assumed he was here to see Sarah. He said no, he was here to see if there was anything he could do for me and to let me know there was no problem delaying Emma's echo. What a comforting thing to do, to come in person. These people had cared about Emma before we knew her and now they included us into that circle. We spoke for a few minutes and discussed Sarah's condition. After he left I felt cared for.

DATE: TUE, 11 OCT 2011 20:31

Hi Again,

Just a quick update to let you know Sarah is improving, if only in small steps. Over the week-end her girth dropped to 41cm. She isn't carrying any extra fluid. Her kidney functions are not normal but well on the way. She is still intubated but is doing some of the breathing on her own. When they x-rayed her lungs, you can now see two! Liver function is still very poor, this makes sense as the cancer has spread to the liver. Docs are hopeful that time and further treatments will take care of this.

Speaking of treatments, I was told that I should expect a minimum of four rounds of chemo and maybe as many as eight. This means, three days of chemo and then three weeks off for each round. At present it is thought Sarah would have to stay in Halifax till the end of treatment so Halifax could be my home well past Christmas. Not sure how Ed and I will work all that out.

Last evening when I was speaking with Dad on the phone he mentioned that he has been having more chest pain of late. When he tries to do anything strenuous he finds himself short of breath and in pain. I decided a quick trip home was in order. I asked friends to drive me to the ferry and came across late this afternoon. I will return tomorrow. It was very hard to leave Sarah but I needed to see Dad and Ed & the girls. Thank-you for all your continued love and support.

Anne

Coming home and leaving Sarah was a *very* difficult thing for me to do! I knew that the hospital staff were well able to look after her. I'd been in the PICU long enough to know that she would get excellent care. What was so hard was that I didn't want Sarah to die without me. If she was going to leave I wanted to be the one to hold her as she went.

Being in the PICU was a challenge for me. In my real life I am a helper. If you have a problem or a need I want to try and help with that. Here I was with pain and suffering all around me and I was not able to do a thing about it. It would not have been appropriate to intervene or interfere. I tried very hard to respect the privacy of the other patients and families as I was entering and exiting the unit. Having said this, some things can't be helped.

One day a teenage girl was brought in. I knew enough by her position and the equipment being used that she was not in good shape. She was not breathing on her own. She was in the bed next to Sarah's. On her second evening in the unit my nurse came to me and said I might want to leave as something bad was going to happen next door. I got up to gather my things but someone came in to talk to me. My leaving was delayed and now I have forever etched in my mind the sobs and heart-wrenching cries of this girl's family. I assumed, though no one told me, that her family had been informed that she would not survive. As soon as I was able to leave I did.

An hour or so later I came back, expecting to see her bed empty but it was not. The next morning and all that day she was still there and her family were with her. She still had a nurse. I was puzzled but did not ask. During the night I was wakened with a call to come to Sarah. I was with her for a few minutes and then was asked to leave the unit while the staff worked on her. What to do? It's not like I could go back to sleep. I decided on a cup of tea and headed for the family kitchen. At three in the morning I expected it to be empty but it was not. There were five adults sitting on the sofa and in the hard chairs. I apologized for disturbing them but they insisted that I come in. I recognized them from the girl's bedside. They asked about Sarah and I told them what was going on. I asked about the girl. "We are waiting for her organs to be harvested," came the response.

Just what is the correct reply in that situation? I surely didn't know! They explained that it may take several more days before her organs could be harvested and they wanted to stay with her until it happened. Two at a time, parents, siblings, cousins, aunts, and uncles were sitting by her bed. It was too much for me to handle. One kind woman made me my tea and as I was leaving she said she would pray for my baby. I returned to the unit and Sarah. At 4:00 am I went back to bed.

After more than three full days. I saw the family walk beside the stretcher as the girl was wheeled to the doors of the OR. It was very moving. I have always believed in organ donation. The theory is fine but watching the reality is quite another thing.

DATE: FRI, 14 OCT 2011 17:00

Hello again,

Just to let you all know Sarah continues to improve. I don't understand all the medical stuff but the staff were quite excited this morning with her blood work—said it was her best single day improvement. She is getting a few mls of food an hour and tolerating this well. She is being weaned off the ventilator. Doc said he thinks they might be able to wean her off the ventilator by Tuesday, at least that is the current goal. She still looks very yellow and liver function is still a problem. Other organs appear to be working ok.

She looks so tiny and I am still not able to hold her. If things keep improving I should be able to hold her by the first of the week. Mum came back with me on Wed and went home today with friends. It was nice to have her here. Dad claims he did not have chest pain—just pain in his chest and tightness!! He does appear to be moving a little slower and resting more often. I am really glad I went home to see him. Emma did not seem very pleased to see me and I only held her a small amount. I am glad she is so attached to Ed. She and I will have to get to know each other when I can go home. Gracie was glad to see me and we had a good time. Gracie has my determined personality—not sure how that happened! Thanks again for all your caring and support. God is good. Love
　Anne

While Mom was visiting we went shopping for some wool. I started knitting an afghan. It was a nice change from sitting doing sudoko. I had already gone through one sudoko book and was working on my second! I thought I would save the afghan for Sarah and give it to her when she is older. I can tell her it was knit with love and prayers for her!

After Sarah shed all the extra fluid she looked sooooooo tiny. I found it hard to look at her and wondered how she would survive. I commented to one nurse that she would make a good poster child for famine relief, with her tiny limbs and swollen belly. Later that day (Sunday)I was sitting at Smitty's trying to make myself eat. I took out my Bible and not knowing where to turn I read Psalm 33. Ed and I love this one. As I was reading, verses 18 & 19 jumped out at me.

"But the eyes of the Lord are on those who fear him, on those whose hope is in his unfailing love, to deliver them from death and keep them alive in famine."

Was God telling me he was going to bring Sarah through this 'famine,' and keep her alive? Was he reminding me of his unfailing love? That was the message that I got.

DATE: MON, 17 OCT 2011 15:25

We have had a few inquiries today so I am sending a short update. Sarah is holding her own. Still on the ventilator. I had a meeting with the docs yesterday afternoon and was told she will not be ready for the second round of chemo on Friday. Not sure when they will do it but she needs to improve a lot more before it happens. They are hopeful she will live but she is still a very sick baby. I came home this morning for one overnight. It is hard to leave Sarah alone but hard not to be with the other girls & Ed. While it is true that I am remaining amazingly peaceful and calm, I do find the time at hospital long and lonely. Again, thanks for all your caring and support. It means a lot to us. God has his hand in all this. Love,

Anne {picture sent with email}

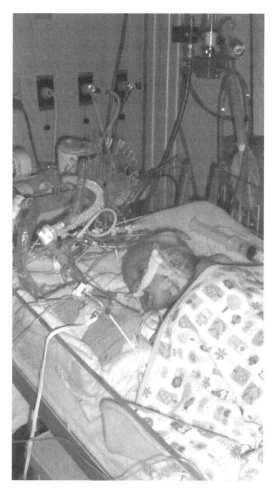

Sarah in the PICU

At morning rounds I spoke with the team about going home for a day. Since I was unable to hold Sarah and she was still sedated they felt that if I was going to go I should go then. When I was leaving I said to the doctor that I was on my way and to please look after my little girl. He replied that there was a 50-50 chance she would be here when I came back. I waited for the smile, or punch line but none came. He was serious. I almost didn't go!

Hi Everyone,

Last evening I spent half an hour typing out an update on Sarah, only to find I had lost the internet and couldn't send it! So let's try this again. Yesterday the word miracle was used three times at rounds. Sarah's blood work is making them all happy as it improves. She had a CT scan that showed the tumor & liver have shrunk a little and the liver looks better. She was taken off the ventilator mid-afternoon. I was able to hold her and give her a bottle . . . twice!! The plan yesterday was for her to move to Six Link, the cancer floor, sometime today.

Well, the difference a day makes. She was not able to tolerate feeding during the night and vomited a few times. Her breathing is labored and uneven. At rounds today the doc said maybe we have taken her off the ventilator too soon and she needs to go back on for a week or so to allow her to rest, and gain weight & strength. Also she is running a temp. Not sure what all this means but she is improving and though very sick we are hopeful we will eventually take her home. I did hold her again today but her breathing seemed worse so we kept it short.

I have received a number of encouraging emails and calls and do appreciate them. It is hard to reply because during the day I like to stay close to Sarah's room so I don't miss all the people coming in to check on her (numerous specialists). The lap top does not get a wireless signal in the PICU. Also I am very poor at navigating around the lap top—used to my key board and mouse I guess. If anyone happens to be in the area we are either on third floor (green elevator) at PICU or 6th Link.

As the shock of what's going on has settled down Ed & I are trying to sort out our new reality. With him off work and home with the other girls and the extra costs with me being here we have been encouraged by the financial gifts and support from family & friends. We praise God for his faithfulness in taking care of us. Dad gave me some books to read and Mom bought me some yarn to knit an afghan so I am managing to fill some of my time with this. The staff are all great, and I am well looked after. God bless,

Anne

Sarah had four PICC (peripherally inserted central catheter) lines. Two in her head, one in her groin, and one in her neck. They are long, tiny, tubes that are threaded through her veins into her chest to get near her heart to allow intravenous access. As you can imagine on one as small as her, it was no easy task to get them in. It had been known for a while that the one in her neck was infected. In weighing the need for access and the risks from infection it was decided that it would stay in but now it had to come out. I was so glad to have such an expert team of people looking after her! They were always balancing the risks and benefits of each procedure.

DATE: MON, 24 OCT 2011 11:13

Hi Everyone,

This is a fun email to write! We have just finished rounds and had the official update on Sarah. She is completely off respiratory support and breathing on her own. She is getting pinker by the day—which means her liver is functioning, if not at 100%, at least somewhat. She still has cancer but it appears that the tumor & liver are shrinking—won't know for sure until next CT scan in about ten days. If the tumor continues to shrink on it's own then docs will just monitor but not do anymore chemo. Sometimes this type of cancer does shrink and clear up on it's own. Still saying we will be here until at least Christmas. She is still on antibiotics, an antifungal, lipids, and diuretics. Feeding at this point is by NG tube until she gets a little stronger though she did take a small amount of milk from a bottle last evening. We will remain in the PICU for at least today. Doc wants to make sure the progress continues before sending her to the cancer floor (6th link). It is also true that the PICU is unusually quiet and the 6th link is crazy busy and has no beds available. Staff all agree her recovery this far is a miracle. When I left her room to come and write this she was cuddled in my Mom's lap, looking wide eyed at Mom and trying to smile! My continued thanks to all for your support & encouragement. Now she is getting better I am restless and wanting to come home! love to all,

Anne (& Sarah)

Sarah continued to improve. Due to an unusually high number of new diagnosis and admissions the cancer floor did not have room for us. On day 30 of our PICU stay a young resident called Eric* came on duty. He had about two hours to get to know the six patients before rounds at 9:00 am. When rounds came to our bed there was the doctor, physiotherapist, dietitian, social worker, charge nurse, primary nurse, and two other residents. Eric gave a run down of what brought Sarah to the ICU and where she was at that moment. The doctor said, "That's fine but let me tell you the rest of the story. When this baby came to us she was not viable. There is no medical reason this baby survived." He didn't sugarcoat it. He had a very comforting yet shocking way of speaking plainly. I jumped in and said there had been many people praying. He replied well that could account for it because from a medical point of view she shouldn't have lived.

On the morning of October 28, Sarah was stable, smiling, and holding her own. There was still no bed on the cancer floor but we didn't need to be in the PICU. At rounds when this was being discussed I suggested we go home. This got a chuckle! Ok so we couldn't go home, what about the QEH. I said if they let me go for a week I promised we would come back for more treatment. Another chuckle all round. At this point Sarah still had one PICC line in her head and she needed an IV running into it continuously. She also had an NG tube because she didn't have the energy yet to take all her nutrition from a bottle. Dr. Litz was back on service and she agreed to allowing us to go to the QEH providing Dr. Morrison would take us. After a few phone calls I learned that we were booked to leave at noon! We would come back to PEI for one week, via EMS. I was packed and ready to go by 11:00 am and watching out my window for the bus! Then I waited. Then I waited some more. Finally at about 5:30 pm our ride arrived and we left for home.

We arrived at the QEH at around 10:00 pm. The staff were great. They settled Sarah and made me tea and toast. It was almost as good as home but not quite. It had been 32 days since we had arrived at the QEH on that sunny, late September day. What a lot had happened since then. The lows, the highs, the agony, the diagnosis, and all the emotions. It had turned into quite an adventure!

The morning after we arrived in Charlottetown Ed and the girls came in for a visit. Emma still didn't want to come to me but she smiled from across the room. I don't blame her—she had only been ours for not quite three months when Sarah and I left. I was so happy she had become attached to Ed. Gracie is the opposite—she wanted to hug me and hold the baby and play, all at once! So nice to have everyone together again!

DATE: SUN, 30 OCT 2011 08:01

Good Morning All,

Sarah and I arrived late Friday evening, by EMS, to the QEH in Charlottetown. The trip went smoothly and the staff here were warm and welcoming. We have a return trip booked for Halifax and the IWK on Monday, November 7th.

Sarah is stable and doing well but she had to come by ambulance because she has a PICC line in her head. At one time she needed four lines but now only one. It has to be kept running so she can receive chemo through it. If it wasn't for this line we could have actually gone home for a few days. When we arrived here Sarah was still being fed through a nasal gastric tube. Yesterday morning she took a bottle and has been doing so every three hours since. If this continues today we will take out the tube!!

Ed and the girls came in for a visit yesterday—what a blessing to all be together again. Gracie was able to hold Sarah and was very pleased to do so. Emma is still the same—she looks at Sarah and points and laughs. Ed is doing a wonderful job caring for the girls. I went out for an hour last evening but other than that am staying here with Sarah. The nurses are great but I don't want to leave her alone.

Before we left Halifax I guess I seemed toooooooo excited—the oncologist took the time to remind me that Sarah is still a very sick child, that she still has cancer, and that she still needs more treatment. I think he thought I was too excited and forgetting the seriousness of Sarah's condition. I assured him I was grounded but just really looking forward to getting closer to my family. I am so thankful that there was no bed available on Sixth Link and we were able to come here.

I will let you know if anything changes but for now we are in a good place, being well cared for. Yesterday a friend stopped by and took my laundry and brought it back clean a few hours later - can it get any better than that!! Someday I am going to write a book about all the ways that God has shown his love and caring through this experience. Regardless of the outcome, God is good and we can trust in his unfailing love. love to all,

Anne

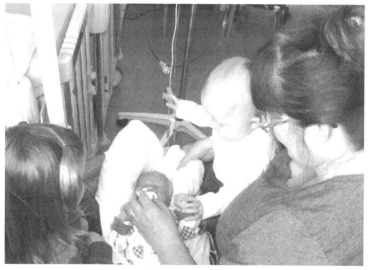

Back with all three of my girls!

It was an important week closer to home and closer to family. I had a chance to spend time with Gracie and Emma. Ed and I managed a meal out together! One of the issues with adoption is attachment. Children need to know that their new families are going to be there for the long haul, day in, and day out. Even though Gracie was with us since birth she has seen a lot of coming and going. She would grieve the loss of foster children when they left our home. Being at the QEH for this week helped her know that I was still her Mom, still loved her, and will always be hers.

With Emma the attachment was not as strong because she had not been with us very long. It had been a good solid three months with lots of time with her but it was still only three months. Plus in that time we also got Sarah. We were so blessed to be able to have Ed at home with her and provide that consistency she needed while I was away. I think Ed and Emma will always have a special bond because of this time.

DATE: FRI, 4 NOV 2011 22:10

Hello all,

Just a short note to say hi and let you know that Sarah and I are booked to go back to the IWK on Monday. We leave at 7am by ambulance. It has been a good week - I have had time with Ed & the girls and even got home for a couple of nights. I plan to go home again tomorrow evening and come back after church on Sunday. Sarah is stable. She was 8lbs 3oz when we came last Friday and this morning she was 8lbs 15 oz. She continues to drink from a bottle and pulled her feeding tube a few days ago and it didn't need to be replaced!! She is smiling and responding as you would expect any 11 week old to do. Her liver function has slipped a bit since we have been here. The plan is for chemo on Tuesday but that will depend on how well she travels and her blood work on Monday pm. I'll keep in touch, God Bless,

Anne & Sarah

Good Morning All,

Sarah and I had a great trip back on Monday. She had a big feed before we left the QEH and slept all the way to the IWK and woke up hungry just as we got here! We are settling into our room (613) here on the 6th link. It is much quieter and less traumatic than the PICU.

We have one more test today, can't remember the name but it is to check out her kidneys, it will take till about noon to finish it and the blood work. Then the docs have a meeting to decide if we proceed with chemo. Chemo is a five hour process all on one day so it may happened today or tomorrow. I did hear a rumor that since everything went so well during our time at home we may get to have another break at the QEH. It depends on how Sarah responds to treatment and if the QEH is willing to take us. They are not used to dealing with babies with cancer so they may say no.

Yesterday I borrowed a musical mobile for Sarah's crib. It has an octopus with fish hanging from it's legs and plays Bach and Mozart. She absolutely loves it! She lay on her back, kicking her legs, swinging her arms, moving her head and cooing and smiling. It was the most response we have had from her. She smiles and coos for the staff and is a real blessing to all. Yesterday as I was rocking her I was overcome with emotion as I realized anew that I get to be a MOM. I am Sarah's Mom! How great is that! After years of being childless I am the mother of three little girls! .... ok, ok, I am going to end this before I get too emotional on you.

God is good. He is faithful to take care of us, if we allow him. Not sure what the end of this journey with Sarah will be but I am very thankful I can trust God throughout it.

Anne

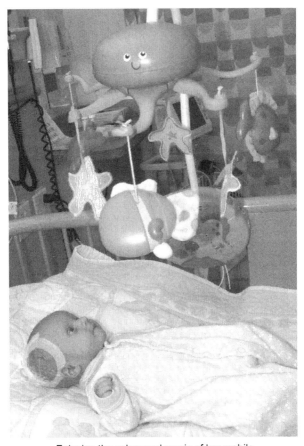
Enjoying the colors and music of her mobile

Being on the Cancer Floor was a whole different experience from being in the PICU. For starters Sarah had her own room. It was a lovely room, nicely decorated with a large window. There was a bed for me and I could stay right with her. But. It was *so* quiet. For the first 48 hours we had to have the door shut and everyone coming in, and me when I'd go out, had to be gowned and gloved to prevent the spread of MRSA. Until Sarah's tests came back clear we were behind closed doors. If I wanted to leave for a meal or a walk or just to see another face, I had to negotiate it with Sarah's nurse. At night the nurses would do one feeding so we would decide which they would do and which I would do. It was just really lonely!

There are so many great things about the IWK. Food is not one of them. On the week-ends the cafeteria is only open from about 11:00 am to 1:00 pm. Not sure what one is supposed to do about breakfast and supper. On holidays it is closed altogether as I discovered on Thanksgiving and Remembrance Day! Part way through my stay I did learn that I could order food from the cafeteria to be sent to my room.

DATE: THU, 10 NOV 2011 20:08

Hello again,

Sarah has not had her chemo yet. The test for her kidneys was delayed until today and it takes a few hours to complete. The result is that her kidneys are only working to about 50-75% of what they should be. Apparently they were damaged when the liver was so big and crushing everything. Over time they will improve. Chemo cocktail has been adjusted to be as easy as possible on them, and will happen first thing tomorrow. If all goes well, and if QEH will take us we could go back as early as Tuesday. Then return here three weeks later. It's still hospital for Sarah & I but far better in Ch'town than here.

We had a great visit with Ed & the girls today. Our friend Lawrence came with them, just for a day trip. There is nothing relaxing about a 13 mth old and 2 1/2 yr old visiting in a hospital but I was still very glad to see them. Gracie seems more settled and Emma will come to me. I will have lots of catching up to do with them when this is over. take care,

Anne & Sarah

93

Sarah's kidneys were not just affected from the liver being so big and crushing them. They were damaged by the first chemo. Also when Sarah was on antibiotics she developed a fungus and the treatment for this was very hard on her kidneys. It's really all a balancing act. If she hadn't had the treatment and drugs she would not have survived. The fact that these caused some damage is of concern but she is still here. She is far above the threshold for dialysis and I have had no indication that they would deteriorate further.

DATE: SUN, 13 NOV 2011 19:51

Hello all,

Sarah had a peaceful day today—she spent it sleeping, drinking, smiling, and cooing. We were able to have two short trips around the hospital and to Tim Hortons in the lobby. I carry Sarah in the snuggly and have a hand free to drag her IV pole.

Friday's Chemo went by with almost no nausea. Yesterday her blood pressure was a concern, that's to do with the damaged kidneys, but today pressure was better. I have been a little weepy and lonely the past few days so I decided this morning to go to church. The nurses suggested a church nearby. One of the first people I saw when I walked in was our friend, Ella. She introduced me to some people and I had a really good time. This afternoon, one of the women I met came over to visit.

It is so different being on this floor after the PICU. There were always people around when I was there. Here I spend most of my time in Sarah's room, by myself. I negotiate with the nurses when is a good time to have a break. I need to plan in advance. Tomorrow a friend is taking me to lunch and I'm really looking forward to that. So that's us. Thanks for all the emails and calls. Thanks for all the help with Ed & the girls. We are truly loved and cared for by you all!

Anne & Sarah

How I ended up at that particular church was due to one of the nurses. She came in the room while I was looking on line and I asked her about an address. She replied that if I was looking for a church I needed to talk to Rachel*, she would know. She sent Rachel in and we talked for a couple of minutes about churches and my background and then she recommended First Congregational Church.

I was a little late getting ready so I took a taxi and arrived just when the music started. There were about 120 people of all ages and mixed races. As I slipped into a seat at the back the woman next to me introduced herself. Turns out she was an RN and later she offered to sit with Sarah so I could have more breaks. As I looked around the meeting room I saw Ella, an older woman who has been in our home and we have known for years. After the service I stayed for a social time. I felt as if God had hand picked the place, just for me!

DATE: MON, 14 NOV 2011 22:33

Just a quick note to let you know that Sarah & I are returning to Charlottetown to the QEH, tomorrow. It is expected that we will be there for two-three weeks and then back for more chemo before Christmas. It will be good to be closer to home but we are going to have to really limit visitors for the first ten days as she gets over this round of chemo. Great day for us to be going home as it is Ed's birthday! more later,

Anne

One of the great programs at the IWK is the Bravery Bead Program. It is a way to celebrate and recognize the events and procedures a child goes through after diagnosis. In Sarah's case I decided to collect the beads for her so I can use them to tell her story to her later. She has an airplane for her life flight. A pink bear for an ICU admission. A dolphin for a new diagnosis. Three clear beads for radiation. Many stars for things like x-rays and tests. There are beads for blood work, injections, PICC lines, and more. As her collection grew an idea came to mind. I decided to make her a memory quilt. It is several shades of pinks and mauves. In the center panel on the front I sewed my favorite of her sleepers. I used some of the beads to make a necklace for the sleeper and still others for bracelets. The back of the quilt is a blanket given to Sarah by our adoption lawyer. The binding is one picked out by her Daddy.

Sarah's Memory Quilt

It was a fun project to work on and helped pass the time. I will save the rest of the beads for Sarah. When she is old enough she can make herself something from them.

DATE: MON, 21 NOV 2011 09:19

Good Morning Everyone,
Sarah is doing very well. We are at the QEH in Charlottetown. It was expected that her white cell count and platelets, etc would drop 7-10 days after chemo but this did not happen—they only dropped a little. She is eating well, gaining weight (10.8 lbs), smiling, and seems happy and content. Our little miracle!

On Friday evening we were encouraged by a benefit concert organized by our friends. I stayed with Sarah but Ed went and enjoyed the visiting, music and support. Mostly I am staying at the hospital but I have been home for a few short visits. It's hard to leave Sarah but great to see the rest of the family. Today is Ellie's 18th birthday so I am hoping to see her. We still expect to be here until December 5th but since Sarah is doing so well we may go back early to the IWK for assessment. Once Sarah is assessed we will know how much more chemo she needs. God continues to use you all to love and support us. We feel truly blessed. love,
 Anne & Sarah

The benefit concert was a real blessing. People we know well and others we have never met came together to help us. There were singers and performers. There was a fudge and bake sale. There was a huge basket of goodies from local businesses for a raffle. In the midst of our pain and worries our community supported us. We were very thankful!

The weekend before Sarah Anne went to hospital my niece, Sarah Elizabeth came for a visit. It was a fun time. Sarah Elizabeth had not met little Sarah and I was happy to introduce them. Sarah Elizabeth was pleased for me that I was able to breast feed as she knew this was something I had really wanted to do. In the course of the conversation she told me about a Swedish study. Apparently women provided breast milk to a milk bank. Adults having chemotherapy drank 6 oz of breast milk a day and it reduced the side effects from their treatment. Neither of us knew that within a week of that conversation Sarah would have been diagnosed with cancer and have had her first chemotherapy! Sarah was getting breast milk before and after her second treatment and she did have far less side effects than were predicted. I wondered if there was a connection.

DATE: TUE, 29 NOV 2011 18:26

Hi Everyone,

Just thought I send an update on our little one. Sarah has been doing great and continues to gain weight, sleep well, and interact as you would expect of any happy three month old. We expected that her counts (white cell, platelets, etc) would drop last week but they have dipped this week instead. Docs are keeping an eye on her and talking with folk at IWK. At this point we just wait but if they dip lower she will need platelets and possibly a blood transfusion. Our return trip to the IWK is booked for 7:30 am on Monday the 5th. I find myself getting restless and wanting to get back to find out where we go from here and if she needs more treatment now or do we wait.

I am going home tomorrow, Wednesday until Friday morning. I need to spend time with the other girls and Ed. This is a good time for me to leave her as there are student nurses in on Wed. & Thurs. I am feeling torn between staying at the hospital with Sarah and being home with Gracie & Emma.

We have been blessed and encouraged by visits, calls, and cards from all sorts of people—old friends and new ones! We received a very lovely card from a young girl called Victoria. Her Sunday School class had each been given $20 to use to do something good. She sent it to us with a note saying she had heard about Sarah and was praying for us and hoped the $ would help. As someone said, Sarah has brought a lot of people to God in prayer! love, Anne

Just a note or two about the student nurses. During our time at the QEH there were a number of first year students on the floor. They were friendly and eager to help! I felt bad for them because most of the time there were no patients—the ward was almost empty. One evening I invited seven of them into my room to talk about Sarah and our situation. I told them they could ask anything they wanted about stimulating breast milk for adopted children and stage 4S neuroblastoma. We spent an hour or so together and they did ask questions. I figure it is a situation they will not come across often in their careers. A forty-nine year old Mother who stimulated breast milk for her adoptive baby is not an everyday occurrence. There are only about 600 cases of stage 4S neuroblastoma a year in Canada and the United States, combined. It was a chance for me to pass on knowledge and feel useful!

DATE: TUE, 6 DEC 2011 08:41

Hi all, just a quick note to say we are back in Halifax at the IWK. Trip over was great, Sarah seems to enjoy traveling . . . We will spend the next two days having tests and assessments and the decision on more chemo or not will come on Thursday morning. I would really like to take her home on Friday but - if more chemo is needed we will do that . . . In spite of the circumstances I am so enjoying watching Sarah grow and change and respond. She is a very contented and happy baby with a smile for everyone! Anne & Sarah

DATE: WED, 7 DEC 2011 20:31

Sarah is coming home!

Hello everyone. After the tests of this week the oncology doctors met and they have decided that Sarah does not need any more treatment at this time. She still has cancer but the tumor has shrunk and the liver is still affected but less so. We will return in two months for a check-up. As long as the cancer continues to go on it's own we won't have anymore chemo. I am in shock - I had prepared myself for another six weeks of this! Ed is coming over in the morning to get us. We get to go home and be a family again, under one roof! This has been a really long ten weeks but throughout it all I have been so blessed and encouraged. We have had help and offers of help from family, friends, and strangers. I have felt your love and caring, every step of the way. There were times when I was so lonely and someone came by to see me. There were times when I worried about Ed and the girls and I heard of someone dropping off a meal or visiting him. Thank-you all so much for walking this journey with me (us).God is good and faithful. Love, Anne

It was a miserable, wet, cold, windy day but Ed and our friend Lawrence made it over to Halifax in good time. We packed up for what I hoped was the last time, and left the hospital. It was such a thrill to be able to hold Sarah and carry her around without her being connected to an IV and pole! We were free!

As we were leaving the hospital I was very emotional. This had been my home on and off for ten weeks. I thought of all the people who had helped us. The life flight crew who had brought Sarah over from Charlottetown. The emergency team who had received her and cared for her until I arrived. The many doctors who were consulted. All the support staff, social workers, Ronald McDonald Room volunteers, Auxiliary volunteers and the staff of 6th Link. Mostly I was remembering the many staff of the PICU. They were the ones who diligently and professionally cared for Sarah during those critical and crucial early days when it didn't look like she would live. They were the ones who, with caring and gentle support, allowed me to walk this journey beside my daughter. I will never forget them. Sarah would not have lived if it hadn't been for the PICU staff.

How many others have walked this journey before me? How many will walk it in the future? Who will be there to hold them up and support them? I was reminded again of how many people God had brought into my path to ease my pain and help carry my load. My eyes were leaking again, this time with joy.

11. Christmas

For the past 24 years Ed and I have organized a Christmas Dinner at our church. It is one of the highlights of the season for me. This year was particularly special. We often have someone share the Christmas Story or a message but I decided this time I wanted to talk. Here are my notes from what I shared:

Do you know anyone who has had a birthday recently? . . . I know Emily* had one, and Matthew* & Charles*. Some others of you may have birthdays around this time. My friend Margaret used to love being a part of this annual Christmas dinner and her birthday is the 14th. She doesn't live on PEI anymore but I often find myself missing her on this night . . . When we celebrate these birthdays we don't think of the person as a baby but as who they are now. Matthew is no longer the tiny baby he was but rather the teenager we see today . . . As we come together this time of year to celebrate Christmas we often think of Jesus' birth. Of Jesus as the babe in a manger, sent by God. The thing is, Jesus is no longer a baby. He hasn't been for long time. ..... The manger is empty.

Jesus came as a baby to fulfill a promise made by God. ...... Jesus didn't stay a baby. As an adult Jesus spent three years telling anyone who would listen all about His Father,

God. Then, Jesus allowed himself to be put to death on a cross.

Our sins had made a separation between us and God. By allowing himself to die on the cross and providing a way for our sins to be paid for Jesus made it possible to close that separation. But he didn't STAY on the cross. ...... The cross is empty.

Jesus is alive with God. We can know him personally. And He longs to be part of our lives. He can be part of all our joys and all our troubles if we will only let him. .... Recently I have been through an experience that brought new meaning to all this. .... For Ed & I 2011 has been the year of the babies. .... Gracie's adoption was finalized. Emma came to live with us in June, when she was nine months old and on August 18th we welcomed Sarah Anne into our family. What a thrilling year in my life - As long as I can remember I have wanted to be a mom, and now I am! .... There has been lots to celebrate and thank God for!

There has also been lots of uncertainty. .... As most of you know Ed & I have a baby with cancer. .... Yes cancer. It has been a learning curve for me to just say that out loud. On September 27th Sarah was airlifted to the IWK and three days later, on her six week birthday, we were told she has stage4S neuroblastoma. ... Cancer. ....After ten weeks and two days in hospitals she is home again and doing well. The doctors expect her to make a full recovery. For her part she will grow up remembering nothing of what has just happened to her. For me, I will carry the memories for a lifetime. ....

I will carry with me the memory of standing by her bed in the ICU and having Dr. Litz tell me Sarah may not live through the day. .... And the memory of her little body, swollen and stretched. .... And the memory of her little whimpers as the nurse tried to start yet another IV. .....

But, with those memories are many others. Like the day I came out of the ICU after I had just been told Sarah had cancer. I was alone. There was not a single person in the hospital who knew me—or so I thought. As I was leaving the ICU I cried out to God for a familiar face, knowing that there wasn't one—I came down the elevator, headed for outside and ran straight into Kay Gillis. She and her daughter had been there for an appointment and were just leaving. They asked what I was doing there and as I shared what was going on, Kay pulled me into her arms and said. "You need a mother's hug and since your mom isn't here I will have to do," God had heard my plea.

Oct 1st was a bad day. Ed & Ruth had come over with the girls. In the morning Sarah was critical but stable and we decided to do something with Emma & Gracie, so we went to the Halifax Farmer's Market. I wasn't in the mood to shop so I found a place to sit and struck up a conversation with a woman from BC. It was her first visit to the Maritimes. Her friend, formerly from NB was showing her around. She told me she was going somewhere special in the afternoon but couldn't remember where it was. Ed and the girls joined us and then we got a call from the hospital to come right away. So we left the Market and returned to the IWK. At the hospital we were told Sarah probably wouldn't survive the day but maybe radiation would help. We consented to it and Ed & Ruth left to go home. .... There were a couple of problems with doing radiation, first that Sarah could not tolerate to be moved and she needed to go down the block to another hospital. Second that she needed a CT scan to show where to do the radiation and she couldn't tolerate the sedative. It took a while to get the staff together to do the radiation and to move us to the other hospital. At about 2:30 or so the docs and technicians were marveling at the ease at which they did the CT scan and markings. I was thanking God for how well things were going. What I didn't know was the other part of the story. .... When Ed got on the ferry he met the same woman we had seen at the Farmer's Market. She asked about Sarah and when Ed told her she and her husband and friends stopped right there to pray. It was about 2:30 pm.

The amazing thing about the whole ordeal is that for the most part I was peaceful. At one point, when I had been told that Sarah probably wouldn't live I asked God for peace to accept what was going on. I was standing by her crib in the ICU and all of a sudden I knew that it was ok if she died. I felt at peace that if she were to die she would be welcomed into the arms of God and into the arms of those who love us who have gone on before us. It doesn't make sense but it was a peace that came from God.

Sarah was in the ICU for 32 days. The IWK is a teaching hospital so there are always students/ residents, etc around. On day 30 this young resident called Eric came on duty. He had about 2 hours to get to know the six patients before rounds at 9:00 am. When rounds came to our bed—nine people—Eric

106

gave a run down of what had brought Sarah to the ICU and where she was at that moment. The doctor said, that's fine but let me tell you the rest of the story. When this baby came to us she was not viable. There is no medical reason this baby survived. I jumped in and said there have been many people praying. He replied, well, that could account for it because she shouldn't have lived.

Over the ten weeks I was away, time after time God met my needs and gave me a peaceful heart. Unexpectedly people showed up. He sent help for Ed & the girls. He prompted people to give money and help us out with the extra financial burden. I could stand here for the next hour and tell you of all the amazing things that happened. Our daughter has cancer but God has been with us every step of the way........ Yes Jesus WAS the baby in a manger, and yes, Jesus WAS the Jesus of the cross, but HE IS the Jesus of now. The Jesus who is alive and well and wanting to know us. Wanting to have us share the journey of life with him.

Once Sarah was home she continued to improve and grow. Within a short time she was eating well, sleeping well (8 hrs most nights!!), and doing everything you would expect of a four month old. She laughed a lot and hardly cried. We were settling back to being a family. Emma decided that I was ok. It did get a little crazy with three little ones but it was a good kind of crazy!

It was a wonderful Christmas! We had our three girls. The older two enjoyed all the excitement and festivities. Sarah was content to watch and smile and coo. We shared Christmas Day with our children and their birth parents. We

had a meal with my parents and some of my siblings. We were blessed with several large boxes of gifts from anonymous donors so we didn't even have to go shopping!

12. A New Year & A New Chapter

Email updates filled in our family and friends on Sarah in January & February.

DATE: WED, 11 JAN 2012 19:57

Hello all & Happy New Year!
Just wanted to update you on Sarah and how she is. ... Well she is doing great. I took her to the paediatrician in Charlottetown last week and she thought she was doing very well. She said that her liver appears to be of normal size. She is up to 14 1/2 lbs. (She was 6.11 at birth.) She continues to sleep through the night, for which I am very grateful! She smiles, and coos, and shrieks, and is trying to roll over. She had blood work done last week and everything came back good except one thing. That just means she is at a greater risk for infection and has still not fully recovered from her last treatment but the Halifax docs are not concerned.

We confirmed today that she will be going back to Halifax for February 2nd. At that time she will have tests to determine if the cancer is continuing to shrink. If tests show that cancer is not going on it's own we would start two more rounds of treatment the following week but it appears that more treatments will probably not be necessary. Gracie & Emma are healthy, busy, and happy! Gracie likes to read to Sarah. Emma continues to laugh and pat Sarah, as if she was a pet. I trust this finds you all well and enjoying another New Year. Anne

Hello all,

For those of you that Ed did not get to update today I am filling in the details.... Sarah had her tests and doc appointments at the IWK today and she is doing very well. Her liver is back to normal. The tumor on her adrenal gland is very small but still visible. The skin lesions on her head are nothing to worry about and will come and go for the next few months, common in most cases of stage 4S neuroblastoma in children under one. There is no need for further treatments and our next check-up isn't until May!! Docs were very pleased with her weight gain, her development, and overall health.

After our time at the oncology clinic we stopped by the PICU to visit with the staff that had provided such good care of us when she was first diagnosed. I was thrilled to show off a healthy baby and they were thrilled to see her! Nice for them to see how their dedication and hard work paid off.

Thanks to all who prayed us through the storm yesterday - worst weather I have ever driven through. The trip over took an extra two hours because of the conditions. The trip home today was great. This has been quite a journey with Sarah. I feel so blessed to have her. So blessed to have had such support from family, friends and strangers. I have personally grown in my walk with God and pray I will continue to do so through the calm times as well (If raising three under three can be called calm!)Thank-you so much for all your love & caring, Anne & Sarah

On March 2nd, 2012 two really cool things happened. The first was that I turned 50. Yes, it was my birthday and I was a half century old. The second, but more important thing was a phone call from the IWK. Sarah's tests results were back from our Feb 2 visit—Sarah is cancer free! There is no sign of the neuroblastoma. Could you get a better birthday gift than that?

On March 9th we went to court again. This time to finalize the adoptions of Emma and Sarah. It was an emotional day for all of us. Our lawyer teared up as she read her statement to the court. I sat, holding Sarah, realizing that she may not have lived to become truly ours, yet here she was. A few of our close family & friends were able to share the proceedings with us. I was officially the mother of three little girls!

All dressed up for our day in court,
visiting with my parents on the way.

In the spring we were asked by the IWK to participate in a Radioathon to raise money for the IWK. I spoke for about twenty minutes and then this was edited and put with a musical background for broadcast. Doing the interview was not too bad but my eyes did leak. Hearing it a few days later, on air, was really tough! I can't believe I lived that! I was very pleased to help the IWK. We wouldn't have Sarah if they weren't there—it's just that simple.

When we were in the PICU Dr. Litz said we should never put yellow on Sarah. At that time yellow made her jaundice look even worse. In June I found a yellow shirt that looks great on her! It was the shirt worn by the survivors at our local Relay For Life event. I pushed Sarah in her stroller for her survivor lap. At 10 months old she was the youngest participant. I was overwhelmed with all the emotions I felt and the kindness and support of everyone there.

Posing in her yellow shirt!

E

llie continues to drop in and out of our lives. My love for her hasn't changed. In my heart she will always be my girl. I was there in the spring when she graduated from high school. I pray I can continue to be part of all the ups and downs, joys and sorrows, and events of her life.

Gracie is a happy, noisy, inquisitive, and charming three-year-old. She loves to be outside with her Daddy, or Auntie Ruth, or Sam the new puppy. She wants to help with whatever we are doing—unless of course we ask her and then she is "busy right now!" Everyone who comes to the house is asked to read her a book. She is anxious to learn to read herself and asks often to, "do my words please?" I look forward to watching her grow up!

Emma spent a couple of nights in the hospital in the spring. She's back on track and is doing well again. She has learned to walk and is starting to talk. She has no trouble communicating—just talking! She continues to be our smiley girl. She loves people, though she often prefers to interact with them from the safety of Daddy's arms! Some time in the next year or so she will have further heart surgery. She will always have less stamina and endurance than others but she will compensate for that with her intelligence. She loves music and movement. She is an absolute joy to have around!

Sarah is crawling everywhere and getting into everything. She is 24 lbs, one year old, and looks like a sumo wrestler! To look at her and watch her you would never believe she was ever sick. In the next month or so she'll be on her feet and there will be no stopping her. She sleeps well and eats well. She sees her paediatrician every two months and the doctors at the IWK every six months. No one is expecting anything to change but she will be followed like this for the next few years. This year we discovered she loves the beach and water. She is almost always happy and just adapts to whatever situation we put her in. I can't wait for her to talk so she can tell me what's behind all her smiles and cheeky grins!

I am truly a blessed person. I had years of learning and growing through childlessness. Years of enjoying other people's little ones. Now I have time with my own children. Throughout it all God has been faithful and consistent. He has never left me. He is God. For those of us who allow it, He holds us in the palm of His hand and in His heart.

Summer of 2012 – Emma & Sarah with Ed, Gracie with Anne

13. A Note or Two

I have been asked how someone might have helped during the time that I was childless. This is a good question. For me the pain was lessened by other people sharing their children and by my reaching out. I do know some childless women who would have found my choices difficult. I think the key is to ask. Ask if the couple with no children would like to come to the beach with your family. Ask if they would like to share a holiday or a meal. If you offer you give them the opportunity and the choice.

Also, watch what you say. People say the craziest things! Several times over the years well meaning people have asked me why God was taking our babies—how crazy is that! God wasn't taking our babies! We live in a world of cause and effect. If I put my hand in a flame I'll get burnt. If my body doesn't work right I'll not carry a child. God could choose to overrule nature—cause a miracle to happen—but he doesn't always do that. He is God. That is His choice. Other things were said without considering the impact they might have on me. I suffered a lot of pain because I took to heart the thoughtless things that were said to me.

Another thing is to allow parents of miscarriage to talk about their children. Just because my children died does not mean they did not exist. Think about it. Most people know they are pregnant in the first few weeks. They don't go around saying, "Oh I have a blob in my belly." No, they say they are going to have a baby! And most do go on to have a baby. The baby existed right from the start. My babies died but they still existed. Sometimes I just wanted to talk about them. About what I had missed and what I had lost. I did have a couple of good friends who let me talk but for most people it made them uncomfortable.

A question that comes up these days is about fostering and are we still foster parents? The short answer is no. It is policy for foster families to take a break when they have major changes in their lives. Changes like death, illness, birth, adoption, divorce, etc. We knew this, agreed with it, and were not surprised when we were told we would have a one year break from fostering when we adopted Emma. In December, six months into that year we received a letter from Child & Family telling us that as of January we were being closed down. No explanation, just closure. I asked for and got a meeting with the resource social worker but he didn't provide us with anything further, other than to say we are closed. Maybe it was because Sarah was sick, but why not wait the year and see what happened. Maybe it was because someone thought we were too busy. I sure hope not—I know people who have more children than us and both parents work full-time! I can only speculate. My hope was that after Sarah turned one we would be a respite home. A home to give hard working foster parents a much needed break. It didn't happen that way.

I would like to answer another question we are asked and that is in regard to the size of our family. I truly do not believe we will ever have a child younger than Sarah. I am however very interested in offering older children a forever home. Of adding to our family through older child adoption. Will it happen? Who knows. A few years ago it certainly didn't look like our girls would be here. I feel we have the ability and the room in our family for more.

I'd like to add a note here on open adoptions and adopting older children. Even as I sit here writing this I know there are foster children in this province who will "age out of care." They will turn eighteen and have no family. When I have asked about this I have been given several responses. I have been told that no one wants older children, that older children are not able to attach and the adoptions fail, and that the cost is too much. I don't know what the real reasons are. I do know that allowing a child who has lost their first family to just age out of care is a travesty.

I know children who have aged out of care. They have no one. Where do they go for Christmas and holidays? Who do they call to tell when they get a job, lose a job, have a baby, have a great day, have a bad day, or any of the other big or little events of life? They are alone with no connection in a world of people who have connections.

Ed and I would take on the challenges and joys of older child adoption and we know others who would too. It seems this is not encouraged. Why? Yes, it is true that sometimes these matches do not survive but what of the ones who do? Don't all children deserve a chance at a forever family?

As to the idea of open adoptions, why is there so much fear? I once heard a young person puzzle over the idea of closed adoptions. She had been adopted and enjoyed a positive relationship with the parents and her birth parents. Her life was stronger and more solid without the unknown of where she came from. I do realize that in a few cases the adoption needs to be closed for safety reasons but this would not always be the case.

How many children need to grow up in foster care becoming lost young adults with no connections before things change? When are we, as a society and community going to say, every child has the right to a forever family?

15880690R00063

Made in the USA
Charleston, SC
25 November 2012